THE MIGHTY ★GEOGRAPHY★ QUIZ BOOK

Table of Contents

Section 1: Capitals

1. What is the capital city of France?
A) Berlin
B) Paris
C) Madrid
D) Rome

2. Which city is the capital of Japan?
A) Beijing
B) Seoul
C) Tokyo
D) Bangkok

3. Identify the capital city of Canada.
A) Ottawa
B) Vancouver
C) Toronto
D) Montreal

4. What is the capital of Australia?
A) Sydney
B) Melbourne
C) Canberra
D) Brisbane

5. Which of these cities is not a capital of South Africa?
A) Cape Town
B) Bloemfontein
C) Pretoria
D) Johannesburg

6. What is the capital city of the United States?
A) New York
B) Washington D.C.
C) Los Angeles
D) Chicago

7. Which city serves as the capital of the United Kingdom?
A) Paris
B) Edinburgh
C) Dublin
D) London

8. Identify the capital city of Brazil.
A) Brasília
B) Rio de Janeiro
C) São Paulo
D) Salvador

9. What is the capital of Italy?
A) Milan
B) Venice
C) Rome
D) Naples

10. Which of these cities is the capital of India?
A) Mumbai
B) Kolkata
C) New Delhi
D) Bangalore

11. What is the capital city of Germany?
A) Munich
B) Frankfurt
C) Hamburg
D) Berlin

12. Identify the capital city of Egypt.
A) Alexandria
B) Giza
C) Luxor
D) Cairo

13. Which city is the capital of Spain?
A) Barcelona
B) Valencia
C) Seville
D) Madrid

14. What is the capital of Russia?
A) Saint Petersburg
B) Moscow
C) Novosibirsk
D) Yekaterinburg

15. Which of these cities is the capital of China?
A) Shanghai
B) Hong Kong
C) Beijing
D) Guangzhou

16. What is the capital city of Argentina?
A) Buenos Aires
B) Cordoba
C) Rosario
D) Mendoza

17. Identify the capital city of Thailand.
A) Phuket
B) Chiang Mai
C) Pattaya
D) Bangkok

18. Which city is the capital of South Korea?
A) Busan
B) Incheon
C) Daegu
D) Seoul

19. What is the capital of Mexico?
A) Guadalajara
B) Monterrey
C) Mexico City
D) Cancún

20. Which of these cities is the capital of Sweden?
A) Gothenburg
B) Stockholm
C) Malmö
D) Uppsala

21. What is the capital city of Turkey?
A) Istanbul
B) Ankara
C) Izmir
D) Antalya

22. Identify the capital city of Nigeria.
A) Lagos
B) Kano
C) Ibadan
D) Abuja

23. Which city is the capital of Norway?
A) Bergen
B) Trondheim
C) Oslo
D) Stavanger

24. What is the capital of Iran?
A) Shiraz
B) Tabriz
C) Mashhad
D) Tehran

25. Which of these cities is the capital of Indonesia?
A) Bandung
B) Surabaya
C) Jakarta
D) Medan

26. What is the capital city of Kenya?
A) Mombasa
B) Nakuru
C) Nairobi
D) Kisumu

27. Identify the capital city of the Netherlands.
A) Amsterdam
B) Rotterdam
C) Utrecht
D) The Hague

28. Which city is the capital of Malaysia?
A) Kuala Lumpur
B) George Town
C) Ipoh
D) Johor Bahru

29. What is the capital of New Zealand?
A) Auckland
B) Christchurch
C) Wellington
D) Hamilton

30. Which of these cities is the capital of Vietnam?
A) Ho Chi Minh City
B) Da Nang
C) Hanoi
D) Hai Phong

31. What is the capital city of Greece?
A) Thessaloniki
B) Patras
C) Heraklion
D) Athens

32. Identify the capital city of Switzerland.
A) Zurich
B) Geneva
C) Basel
D) Bern

33. Which city is the capital of Portugal?
A) Porto
B) Lisbon
C) Braga
D) Faro

34. Which of these cities is the capital of Saudi Arabia?
A) Jeddah
B) Mecca
C) Medina
D) Riyadh

35. What is the capital city of Belgium?
A) Antwerp
B) Bruges
C) Brussels
D) Ghent

36. Identify the capital city of Colombia.
A) Medellín
B) Cali
C) Cartagena
D) Bogotá

37. Which city is the capital of Peru?
A) Cusco
B) Arequipa
C) Trujillo
D) Lima

38. What is the capital of Poland?
A) Kraków
B) Warsaw
C) Wrocław
D) Gdańsk

39. Which of these cities is the capital of Finland?
A) Turku
B) Tampere
C) Helsinki
D) Oulu

40. What is the capital city of Denmark?
A) Copenhagen
B) Odense
C) Aarhus
D) Aalborg

41. Identify the capital city of the Philippines.
A) Quezon City
B) Davao City
C) Cebu City
D) Manila

42. Which city is the capital of Ireland?
A) Cork
B) Galway
C) Dublin
D) Limerick

43. What is the capital of Bangladesh?
    A) Chittagong
    B) Khulna
    C) Sylhet
    D) Dhaka

44. Which of these cities is the capital of Chile?
    A) Valparaíso
    B) Concepción
    C) Santiago
    D) Antofagasta

45. What is the capital city of Austria?
    A) Graz
    B) Linz
    C) Salzburg
    D) Vienna

46. Identify the capital city of South Sudan.
    A) Wau
    B) Malakal
    C) Juba
    D) Bor

47. What is the capital of Ukraine?
    A) Lviv
    B) Odessa
    C) Kharkiv
    D) Kyiv

48. Which of these cities is the capital of Mongolia?
    A) Ulaanbaatar
    B) Erdenet
    C) Darkhan
    D) Ölgii

49. What is the capital city of Cuba?
A) Santiago de Cuba
B) Camagüey
C) Havana
D) Santa Clara

50. Identify the capital city of Pakistan.
A) Karachi
B) Islamabad
C) Lahore
D) Faisalabad

51. Which city is the capital of Romania?
A) Cluj-Napoca
B) Timișoara
C) Iași
D) Bucharest

52. What is the capital of Nepal?
A) Pokhara
B) Lalitpur
C) Biratnagar
D) Kathmandu

53. Which of these cities is the capital of Hungary?
A) Budapest
B) Szeged
C) Debrecen
D) Bucharest

54. What is the capital city of Slovakia?
A) Košice
B) Prešov
C) Bratislava
D) Žilina

55. Identify the capital city of Croatia.
    A) Split
    B) Zagreb
    C) Rijeka
    D) Dubrovnik

56. Which city is the capital of Belarus?
    A) Gomel
    B) Mogilev
    C) Vitebsk
    D) Minsk

57. What is the capital of Sri Lanka?
    A) Kandy
    B) Galle
    C) Colombo
    D) Jaffna

58. Which of these cities is the capital of the Czech Republic?
    A) Brno
    B) Ostrava
    C) Plzeň
    D) Prague

59. What is the capital city of Morocco?
    A) Casablanca
    B) Marrakesh
    C) Rabat
    D) Fes

60. Identify the capital city of Fiji.
    A) Nadi
    B) Lautoka
    C) Suva
    D) Labasa

61. Which city is the capital of Bulgaria?
A) Varna
B) Plovdiv
C) Burgas
D) Sofia

62. What is the capital of Lebanon?
A) Tripoli
B) Sidon
C) Tyre
D) Beirut

63. Which of these cities is the capital of Jordan?
A) Zarqa
B) Amman
C) Aqaba
D) Irbid

64. What is the capital city of Serbia?
A) Belgrade
B) Niš
C) Kragujevac
D) Novi Sad

65. Identify the capital city of Estonia.
A) Tallinn
B) Narva
C) Vyborg
D) Tartu

66. Which city is the capital of Lithuania?
A) Kaunas
B) Klaipėda
C) Šiauliai
D) Vilnius

67. Which of these cities is the capital of Bosnia and Herzegovina?
    A) Banja Luka
    B) Mostar
    C) Tuzla
    D) Sarajevo

68. What is the capital city of Uruguay?
    A) Montevideo
    B) Salto
    C) Paysandú
    D) Rivera

69. Identify the capital city of Kazakhstan.
    A) Almaty
    B) Shymkent
    C) Nur-Sultan
    D) Karaganda

70. What is the capital of Syria?
    A) Aleppo
    B) Homs
    C) Latakia
    D) Damascus

71. Which of these cities is the capital of Uzbekistan?
    A) Samarkand
    B) Bukhara
    C) Namangan
    D) Tashkent

72. Identify the capital city of Iceland.
    A) Akureyri
    B) Keflavík
    C) Reykjavík
    D) Hafnarfjörður

73. What is the capital of Armenia?
    A) Gyumri
    B) Vanadzor
    C) Yerevan
    D) Ejmiatsin

74. Which of these cities is the capital of Georgia (country)?
    A) Batumi
    B) Kutaisi
    C) Rustavi
    D) Tbilisi

75. What is the capital city of Qatar?
    A) Al Rayyan
    B) Doha
    C) Al Wakrah
    D) Lusail

76. Identify the capital city of Laos.
    A) Luang Prabang
    B) Savannakhet
    C) Pakse
    D) Vientiane

77. Which city is the capital of Bahrain?
    A) Muharraq
    B) Riffa
    C) Manama
    D) Isa Town

78. What is the capital of Albania?
    A) Durrës
    B) Vlorë
    C) Shkodër
    D) Tirana

79. Which of these cities is the capital of Slovenia?
    A) Maribor
    B) Kranj
    C) Ljubljana
    D) Celje

80. What is the capital city of Cyprus?
    A) Limassol
    B) Larnaca
    C) Paphos
    D) Nicosia

81. Identify the capital city of Malta.
    A) Mdina
    B) Valletta
    C) Sliema
    D) Rabat

82. Which city is the capital of Luxembourg?
    A) Esch-sur-Alzette
    B) Dudelange
    C) Luxembourg City
    D) Differdange

83. What is the capital of Oman?
    A) Salalah
    B) Sohar
    C) Nizwa
    D) Muscat

84. Which of these cities is the capital of Azerbaijan?
    A) Ganja
    B) Sumqayit
    C) Baku
    D) Lankaran

85. Identify the capital city of Paraguay.
    A) Ciudad del Este
    B) San Lorenzo
    C) Luque
    D) Asunción

86. Which city is the capital of Zambia?
    A) Ndola
    B) Kitwe
    C) Lusaka
    D) Livingstone

87. Which of these cities is the capital of Ghana?
    A) Kumasi
    B) Accra
    C) Sekondi-Takoradi
    D) Tamale

88. What is the capital city of Bolivia?
    A) Santa Cruz de la Sierra
    B) El Alto
    C) La Paz
    D) Sucre

89. Which city is the capital of the Dominican Republic?
    A) Santiago
    B) La Romana
    C) San Cristóbal
    D) Santo Domingo

90. What is the capital of Libya?
    A) Benghazi
    B) Misrata
    C) Tripoli
    D) Bayda

91. Which of these cities is the capital of Ecuador?
A) Guayaquil
B) Cuenca
C) Santo Domingo
D) Quito

92. What is the capital city of Portugal?
A) Porto
B) Lisbon
C) Braga
D) Faro

93. Which city is the capital of Tanzania?
A) Dodoma
B) Mwanza
C) Arusha
D) Zanzibar City

94. Which of these cities is the capital of Latvia?
A) Daugavpils
B) Liepāja
C) Jelgava
D) Riga

95. What is the capital city of Costa Rica?
A) Alajuela
B) Heredia
C) Cartago
D) San José

96. Identify the capital city of El Salvador.
A) Santa Ana
B) San Miguel
C) San Salvador
D) Soyapango

97. Which city is the capital of Honduras?
A) San Pedro Sula
B) La Ceiba
C) Choloma
D) Tegucigalpa

98. What is the capital of Burkina Faso?
A) Bobo-Dioulasso
B) Koudougou
C) Ouagadougou
D) Banfora

99. Which of these cities is the capital of Cameroon?
A) Douala
B) Yaoundé
C) Garoua
D) Bamenda

100. What is the capital of California?
A) Los Angeles
B) San Francisco
C) Sacramento
D) San Diego

101. Which city is the capital of Texas?
A) Houston
B) Austin
C) Dallas
D) San Antonio

102. Identify the capital of Florida.
A) Miami
B) Orlando
C) Tallahassee
D) Tampa

103. What is the capital of New York?
A) New York City
B) Buffalo
C) Albany
D) Rochester

104. Choose the capital of Illinois.
A) Chicago
B) Springfield
C) Naperville
D) Peoria

105. Which of these cities is the capital of Colorado?
A) Denver
B) Colorado Springs
C) Boulder
D) Aspen

106. Identify the capital of Washington state.
A) Seattle
B) Spokane
C) Olympia
D) Tacoma

107. What is the capital of Massachusetts?
A) Boston
B) Cambridge
C) Salem
D) Worcester

108. Select the capital of Arizona.
A) Tucson
B) Phoenix
C) Mesa
D) Scottsdale

109. What is the capital of Georgia?
A) Atlanta
B) Savannah
C) Athens
D) Macon

110. Choose the capital of Pennsylvania.
A) Philadelphia
B) Pittsburgh
C) Harrisburg
D) Lancaster

111. Which city is the capital of Ohio?
A) Cleveland
B) Cincinnati
C) Toledo
D) Columbus

112. Identify the capital of Michigan.
A) Detroit
B) Grand Rapids
C) Lansing
D) Flint

113. What is the capital of Oregon?
A) Portland
B) Eugene
C) Salem
D) Bend

114. Select the capital of Louisiana.
A) New Orleans
B) Baton Rouge
C) Shreveport
D) Lafayette

Section 2: Rivers & Lakes

115. The Ganges River is most associated with which country?
A) China
B) India
C) Nepal
D) Bangladesh

116. What river runs through Paris?
A) Seine
B) Danube
C) Rhine
D) Thames

117. Lake Victoria is shared by three countries. Which of the following is NOT one of them?
A) Kenya
B) Ethiopia
C) Tanzania
D) Uganda

118. Which river forms part of the border between the United States and Mexico?
A) Colorado River
B) Missouri River
C) Mississippi River
D) Rio Grande

119. The Danube River empties into which body of water?
A) North Sea
B) Adriatic Sea
C) Baltic Sea
D) Black Sea

120. Which of the following rivers is found in South America?
   A) Orinoco
   B) Mekong
   C) Volga
   D) Euphrates

121. Lake Tahoe is located on the border of which two U.S. states?
   A) Nevada and Utah
   B) California and Nevada
   C) Oregon and California
   D) Arizona and Nevada

122. The Yellow River, also known as Huang He, is primarily located in which country?
   A) Japan
   B) China
   C) Vietnam
   D) South Korea

123. Which river is known as the "Father of African Rivers"?
   A) Congo River
   B) Nile River
   C) Niger River
   D) Zambezi River

124. Lake Superior is one of the Great Lakes in North America. Which of the following states does NOT border it?
   A) Illinois
   B) Michigan
   C) Minnesota
   D) Wisconsin

125. The Volga River flows into which body of water?
   A) Baltic Sea
   B) Black Sea
   C) Caspian Sea
   D) Sea of Azov

126. Which river is often referred to as the most important waterway in Southeast Asia?
A) Yangtze River
B) Irrawaddy River
C) Ganges River
D) Mekong River

127. Lake Baikal is in which country?
A) Mongolia
B) Russia
C) China
D) Kazakhstan

128. What is the primary river flowing through Baghdad?
A) Euphrates
B) Tigris
C) Jordan
D) Nile

129. Which Canadian province is home to the Great Bear Lake?
A) British Columbia
B) Alberta
C) Northwest Territories
D) Ontario

130. The Rhine River flows through several countries. Which of the following is NOT one of them?
A) Germany
B) France
C) Switzerland
D) Spain

131. What is the largest lake in Central America?
A) Lake Atitlán
B) Lake Nicaragua
C) Lake Managua
D) Lake Gatun

132. The Amazon River discharges the most water of any river in the world. In which ocean does it end?
A) Atlantic Ocean
B) Pacific Ocean
C) Indian Ocean
D) Southern Ocean

133. Which river is known for its historical significance in the development of the United States' West?
A) Missouri River
B) Colorado River
C) Mississippi River
D) Ohio River

134. What is the largest freshwater lake by surface area in the world?
A) Lake Baikal
B) Caspian Sea
C) Lake Victoria
D) Lake Superior

135. The river famously known for flowing backwards due to engineering is the:
A) Thames River
B) Danube River
C) Seine River
D) Chicago River

136. Which river forms much of the border between Zambia and Zimbabwe?
A) Congo River
B) Zambezi River
C) Limpopo River
D) Niger River

137. Dead Sea, the saltiest lake in the world, is bordered by Jordan and which other country?
A) Israel
B) Egypt
C) Lebanon
D) Syria

138. The source of the Blue Nile, a tributary of the Nile River, is in which country?
A) Egypt
B) Sudan
C) Ethiopia
D) Uganda

139. Lake Titicaca, the highest navigable lake in the world, is located between which two countries?
A) Argentina and Chile
B) Bolivia and Peru
C) Colombia and Ecuador
D) Brazil and Paraguay

140. What river flows through Cairo?
A) Niger River
B) Nile River
C) Congo River
D) Zambezi River

141. Which river is known as the 'Sorrow of China' due to its frequent flooding?
A) Yangtze River
B) Pearl River
C) Yellow River (Huang He)
D) Mekong River

142. Tonlé Sap, a unique seasonal lake, is a prominent feature in which country?
A) Vietnam
B) Laos
C) Thailand
D) Cambodia

143. The Yenisei River primarily flows through which country?
A) Mongolia
B) Russia
C) China
D) Kazakhstan

144. Which river is known for forming the Grand Canyon?
A) Colorado River
B) Mississippi River
C) Rio Grande
D) Yukon River

145. The Murray River is the longest river in which country?
A) Canada
B) Australia
C) New Zealand
D) South Africa

146. Which of these rivers flows through the most countries?
A) Danube
B) Amazon
C) Nile
D) Yangtze

147. Lake Baikal holds approximately what percentage of the world's fresh surface water?
A) 9%
B) 13%
C) 16%
D) 20%

148. The Indus River is crucial to which country's agriculture?
A) India
B) Pakistan
C) China
D) Afghanistan

149. Which lake in North America is known for being one of the Great Salt Lakes?
A) Lake Erie
B) Lake Ontario
C) Great Salt Lake
D) Lake Michigan

150. The Mekong River Delta is a vital region for which country?
A) China
B) Thailand
C) Vietnam
D) Cambodia

151. What is the primary outflow of Lake Geneva?
A) Rhine River
B) Rhône River
C) Arve River
D) Po River

152. The Tigris River mainly runs through which country?
A) Iraq
B) Iran
C) Turkey
D) Syria

153. Which lake is famously known as the source of the river Nile?
A) Lake Tanganyika
B) Lake Albert
C) Lake Tana
D) Lake Victoria

154. The Ural River flows into which sea?
A) Caspian Sea
B) Black Sea
C) Baltic Sea
D) Aral Sea

155. Loch Ness is located in which country?
A) Ireland
B) Scotland
C) England
D) Norway

156. Which African river is the longest tributary of the Congo River?
A) Kasai River
B) Ubangi River
C) Lualaba River
D) Lomami River

157. Which of these countries does not border Lake Chad?
A) Niger
B) Nigeria
C) Cameroon
D) Ethiopia

158. The Ganges River is sacred in which religion?
A) Islam
B) Christianity
C) Hinduism
D) Buddhism

159. Lake Winnipeg is a large freshwater lake located in which Canadian province?
A) Ontario
B) Quebec
C) British Columbia
D) Manitoba

160. The Potomac River is famously associated with which U.S. city?

A) New York City
B) Chicago
C) Washington, D.C.
D) Los Angeles

Section 3: Mountains & Mountain Ranges

161. The Andes Mountain range is located in which continent?
A) Asia
B) South America
C) Africa
D) North America

162. The Rocky Mountains are primarily located in which two countries?
A) Canada and the United States
B) United States and Mexico
C) Canada and Russia
D) Russia and the United States

163. What is the primary cause for the formation of mountains?
A) Meteor impacts
B) Erosion by wind and water
C) Movement of tectonic plates
D) Volcanic activity

164. Which mountain range is known as the "Roof of the World"?
A) The Alps
B) The Himalayas
C) The Rockies
D) The Andes

165. Mount Fuji is an iconic symbol of which country?
A) China
B) Japan
C) South Korea
D) Nepal

166. The Appalachian Mountains are primarily located in which country?
A) Canada
B) Russia
C) Mexico
D) United States

167. What is the second-highest mountain in the world?
A) K2
B) Kangchenjunga
C) Lhotse
D) Makalu

168. Which mountain range separates Europe from Asia?
A) The Ural Mountains
B) The Alps
C) The Himalayas
D) The Pyrenees

169. Mount Elbrus, the highest peak in Europe, is part of which mountain range?
A) The Alps
B) The Caucasus Mountains
C) The Pyrenees
D) The Carpathian Mountains

170. The Drakensberg Mountains are in which country?
A) Australia
B) Switzerland
C) Canada
D) South Africa

171. Which is the longest mountain range in the world?
A) The Andes
B) The Himalayas
C) The Rockies
D) The Alps

172. What type of mountain is formed primarily by volcanic activity?
A) Fold Mountains
B) Block Mountains
C) Volcanic Mountains
D) Plateau Mountains

173. Mount Vesuvius is in which country?
A) Greece
B) Italy
C) Spain
D) France

174. The Atlas Mountains are found in which part of Africa?
A) Southern Africa
B) Eastern Africa
C) Northern Africa
D) Western Africa

175. Aconcagua, the highest mountain outside of Asia, is part of which mountain range?
A) The Rockies
B) The Andes
C) The Alps
D) The Himalayas

176. What is the highest mountain in North America?
A) Mount McKinley
B) Mount Logan
C) Mount Saint Elias
D) Pico de Orizaba

177. The famous K2 Mountain is part of which mountain range?
A) The Alps
B) The Andes
C) The Himalayas
D) The Karakoram

178. The Sierra Nevada Mountain range is primarily located in which country?
A) Spain
B) United States
C) Mexico
D) Canada

179. Which mountain is the highest point in the Antarctic?
A) Mount Erebus
B) Vinson Massif
C) Mount Sidley
D) Pico de Orizaba

180. The Pyrenees Mountain range forms a natural border between which two countries?
A) France and Spain
B) Italy and Switzerland
C) Norway and Sweden
D) Austria and Germany

181. Mount Kilimanjaro is unique for having what near its summit?
A) A crater lake
B) A rainforest
C) Glaciers
D) Desert

182. The Tatra Mountains is on the border of which two countries?
A) Poland and Slovakia
B) Switzerland and Italy
C) France and Germany
D) Austria and Slovenia

183. Which mountain range is known as the backbone of Italy?
A) The Dolomites
B) The Apennines
C) The Alps
D) The Carpathians

184. The famous Mount Rushmore is in which mountain range?
A) The Rockies
B) The Sierra Nevada
C) The Black Hills
D) The Appalachians

185. Which mountain in the Himalayas is known for its distinct pyramid shape?
A) Mount Everest
B) K2
C) Lhotse
D) Ama Dablam

186. The Great Dividing Range is a major mountain range in which country?
A) Canada
B) Australia
C) United States
D) South Africa

187. Mount Olympus, known in mythology as the home of the Greek gods, is in which country?
A) Italy
B) Greece
C) Turkey
D) Cyprus

188. The Carpathian Mountains span across several countries in Eastern Europe. Which of these countries does not have part of the Carpathians?
A) Romania
B) Poland
C) Hungary
D) Bulgaria

189. Which mountain is known as the highest point in the British Isles?
A) Snowdon
B) Ben Nevis
C) Scafell Pike
D) Mount Snowdon

190. The Caucasus Mountains form a border between Europe and Asia. Which of these peaks is the highest in the range?
A) Mount Elbrus
B) Dykh-Tau
C) Mount Kazbek
D) Shkhara

191. Mount Ararat, famous in biblical lore, is in which modern-day country?
A) Iran
B) Turkey
C) Armenia
D) Iraq

192. Which mountain range in North America is known for its extensive system of national parks and protected areas?
A) The Appalachian Mountains
B) The Rocky Mountains
C) The Sierra Nevada
D) The Cascades

193. What is the name of the mountain range that extends along the western coast of South America?
A) The Andes
B) The Rockies
C) The Sierra Madre
D) The Cordilleras

194. Mount Logan is in which territory?
A) Yukon
B) Northwest Territories
C) British Columbia
D) Nunavut

195. The Blue Mountains are a notable range located in which country?
A) Canada
B) Australia
C) United States
D) New Zealand

196. The Alps span across several European countries. Which of these countries does NOT contain a portion of the Alps?
A) Switzerland
B) Italy
C) Germany
D) Belgium

197. Which mountain is known for being the highest peak in South America?
A) Mount Aconcagua
B) Mount Fitz Roy
C) Nevado Sajama
D) Huascarán

198. Mount Kosciuszko, often considered the highest mountain in Australia, is part of which range?
A) The Great Dividing Range
B) The Flinders Range
C) The Snowy Mountains
D) The MacDonnell Ranges

199. The Urals, one of the oldest mountain ranges in the world, are primarily located in which country?
A) Kazakhstan
B) Mongolia
C) China
D) Russia

200. The Mauna Kea, a dormant volcano, is located on which island?
A) Maui
B) Oahu
C) Big Island of Hawaii
D) Kauai

201. Which mountain range in Africa is known as the "Mountains of the Moon"?
A) The Drakensberg
B) The Atlas Mountains
C) The Ruwenzori Range
D) The Simien Mountains

202. Mount McKinley, also known as Denali, is in which U.S. state?
A) Alaska
B) Washington
C) Montana
D) California

203. The Hindu Kush Mountain range is primarily located in which two countries?
A) India and Nepal
B) Pakistan and Afghanistan
C) China and Bhutan
D) Myanmar and Thailand

204. The "Table Mountain" is a prominent landmark in which city?
A) Sydney
B) Cape Town
C) Vancouver
D) Rio de Janeiro

205. Mont Blanc, borders which two countries?
A) France and Switzerland
B) Switzerland and Italy
C) France and Italy
D) Italy and Austria

206. The Sierra Madre Mountain range is primarily located in which country?
A) United States
B) Colombia
C) Guatemala
D) Mexico

207. Mount Fuji is classified as what type of volcano?
A) Shield volcano
B) Lava dome
C) Cinder cone volcano
D) Stratovolcano

208. What is the highest peak in the Appalachian Mountains?
A) Clingmans Dome
B) Mount Mitchell
C) Mount Washington
D) Spruce Knob

209. K2 is also known by what another name?
A) Savage Mountain
B) Godwin-Austen
C) Broad Peak
D) Gasherbrum

210. What is the tallest mountain in South America?
A) Mount Aconcagua
B) Ojos del Salado
C) Huascaran
D) Monte Pissis

211. Mount Elbrus, Europe's highest peak, is part of which mountain range?
A) The Alps
B) The Pyrenees
C) The Carpathians
D) The Caucasus

212. Which is the highest peak in New Zealand?
A) Mount Cook (Aoraki)
B) Mount Tasman
C) Mount Ruapehu
D) Mount Aspiring

213. What is the highest peak in Antarctica?
A) Mount Vinson
B) Mount Kirkpatrick
C) Mount Erebus
D) Mount Sidley

214. Denali is located in which U.S. state?
A) Washington
B) Alaska
C) Colorado
D) Montana

215. What is the highest peak in the Atlas Mountains?
A) M'Goun
B) Toubkal
C) Ras Dashen
D) Mount Kenya

216. The highest peak in the Rocky Mountains is?
A) Mount McKinley
B) Mount Rainier
C) Mount Whitney
D) Mount Elbert

217. Mount Everest is part of which mountain range?
A) The Alps
B) The Andes
C) The Himalayas
D) The Karakoram

218. What is the highest peak in Africa?
A) Mount Kilimanjaro
B) Mount Kenya
C) Ras Dashen
D) Mount Meru

219. The highest peak in the Alps is?
A) Mont Blanc
B) Matterhorn
C) Dufourspitze
D) Jungfrau

220. Puncak Jaya, also known as Carstensz Pyramid, is the highest peak in which continent?
A) Asia
B) Australia
C) South America
D) Oceania

221. Mount Fuji, a symbol of Japan, is located on which island?
A) Hokkaido
B) Honshu
C) Kyushu
D) Shikoku

222. Which is the highest peak in the Andes Mountains?
A) Ojos del Salado
B) Monte Pissis
C) Aconcagua
D) Huascaran

223. The highest peak in the Sierra Nevada range is?
A) Mount Whitney
B) Mount Shasta
C) Mount Rainier
D) Mount Hood

224. Mount Kilimanjaro is known for its three volcanic cones. Which is not one of them?
A) Kibo
B) Mawenzi
C) Shira
D) Meru

225. Which mountain is the highest point in the contiguous United States?
A) Mount Whitney
B) Mount Elbert
C) Mount Rainier
D) Mount McKinley

Section 4: Climate Zones

226. What climate zone is characterized by high temperatures and heavy rainfall throughout the year?
A) Desert
B) Tundra
C) Tropical Rainforest
D) Temperate

227. Which climate zone is known for having four distinct seasons, including a cold winter and a warm summer?
A) Mediterranean
B) Temperate
C) Polar
D) Tropical

228. In which climate zone would you find the majority of the world's deserts?
A) Subtropical
B) Tropical
C) Temperate
D) Arctic

229. The Tundra climate zone is characterized by:
A) High levels of year-round snowfall
B) Constantly freezing temperatures
C) Hot summers and short cold winters
D) Low temperatures and sparse vegetation

230. What feature is most characteristic of a Mediterranean climate?
A) Tropical temperature with low rainfall
B) Constantly high humidity and rainfall
C) Arid
D) Hot, dry summers and mild, wet winters

231. Which of the following climate zones generally has the greatest extreme temperature variations between day and night?
A) Tropical Rainforest
B) Desert
C) Tundra
D) Temperate

232. Polar climates are generally found in which areas of the Earth?
A) Equatorial regions
B) Close to the Tropics of Cancer and Capricorn
C) Near the Arctic and Antarctic Circles
D) Inland areas far from the sea

233. What characteristic is typical of a Continental climate?
A) High humidity and frequent rain
B) Mild winters and hot summers
C) Severe winters and warm summers
D) Uniform temperature & precipitation throughout the year

234. In which climate zone would you most likely find permafrost?
A) Continental
B) Tundra
C) Temperate
D) Subarctic

235. The Monsoon climate is characterized by:
A) Dry conditions throughout the year
B) Heavy rain in the summer and dry weather in the winter
C) Constantly cold temperatures
D) Mild and wet conditions year-round

236. Steppe climates are characterized by:
A) High humidity and frequent rain
B) Hot, dry summers and cold winters
C) Constantly freezing temperatures
D) Uniform temperatures and high precipitation all year

237. Which climate zone is typically found at the highest latitudes?
    A) Tropical
    B) Temperate
    C) Polar
    D) Desert

238. What type of vegetation is most commonly found in the Mediterranean climate zone?
    A) Dense rainforests
    B) Broadleaf forests
    C) Shrubs and woodlands
    D) Tundra vegetation

239. The Savanna climate is characterized by:
    A) Heavy snowfall and freezing temperatures
    B) Prolonged dry seasons and short wet seasons
    C) Constant rain and high humidity
    D) Four seasons

240. Which climate zone typically contains the largest biodiversity?
    A) Desert
    B) Tundra
    C) Tropical Rainforest
    D) Polar

241. What distinguishes a Humid Subtropical climate?
    A) Very dry conditions year-round
    B) Warm to hot summers and cool to mild winters
    C) Constantly cold temperatures with little precipitation
    D) Uniform climate conditions throughout the year

242. Which climate zone is most likely to experience midnight sun phenomena?
    A) Tropical
    B) Desert
    C) Temperate
    D) Polar

243. Which climate zone dominates most of central Canada?
A) Tropical
B) Continental
C) Mediterranean
D) Subarctic

244. The climate of Southern California is typically:
A) Desert
B) Mediterranean
C) Oceanic
D) Tropical

245. Greenland is primarily characterized by which climate zone?
A) Polar
B) Tundra
C) Continental
D) Subarctic

246. The majority of Australia falls under which climate zone?
A) Mediterranean
B) Tropical
C) Temperate
D) Desert

247. The climate of the Himalayan region is best described as:
A) Desert
B) Polar
C) Highland
D) Continental

248. What type of climate is most common in the United Kingdom?
A) Continental
B) Mediterranean
C) Oceanic
D) Highland

249. The south-eastern United States is predominantly which
    climate zone?
    A) Humid Subtropical
    B) Continental
    C) Tropical
    D) Mediterranean

250. Tokyo, Japan, is primarily in which climate zone?
    A) Continental
    B) Humid Subtropical
    C) Oceanic
    D) Subarctic

251. The climate of the Andes Mountains can be best described as:
    A) Highland
    B) Tropical Rainforest
    C) Desert
    D) Temperate

252. Which climate zone characterizes most of the Scandinavian
    Peninsula?
    A) Polar
    B) Oceanic
    C) Subarctic
    D) Tropical

253. What is the dominant climate zone of the Nile River Valley?
    A) Desert
    B) Temperate
    C) Tropical
    D) Subarctic

254. The climate of the Alps is typically:
    A) Highland
    B) Desert
    C) Temperate
    D) Polar

255. The majority of India's climate can be classified as:
A) Desert
B) Tundra
C) Monsoon
D) Continental

256. What is the predominant climate zone in the Atacama Desert?
A) Polar
B) Temperate
C) Desert
D) Tropical

257. The Patagonia region in South America is primarily known for which climate?
A) Humid Subtropical
B) Desert
C) Polar
D) Oceanic

258. Which climate zone is predominant in the Congo Basin?
A) Desert
B) Tundra
C) Tropical Rainforest
D) Temperate

259. The climate of most of the Russian territory is classified as:
A) Mediterranean
B) Subarctic
C) Tropical
D) Desert

260. What type of climate is prevalent in the North African region?
A) Polar
B) Desert
C) Oceanic
D) Humid Subtropical

Section 5: Cultural Geography

261. Which country is known for its unique practice of 'siesta', a midday nap?
A) Italy
B) Spain
C) Portugal
D) Greece

262. The kimono is a traditional form of clothing associated with which country?
A) China
B) Japan
C) Korea
D) Vietnam

263. In which country would you find the architectural style known as 'Fachwerkhaus'?
A) France
B) Germany
C) Switzerland
D) Austria

264. 'Bollywood' is a film industry based in which country?
A) Pakistan
B) Bangladesh
C) India
D) Nepal

265. The concept of 'hygge', emphasizing coziness and comfort, originates from which culture?
A) Swedish
B) Norwegian
C) Danish
D) Finnish

266. Which city is renowned for its Carnival, featuring samba dancing and elaborate costumes?
A) Rio de Janeiro
B) Buenos Aires
C) Havana
D) Mexico City

267. 'Haka', a traditional war dance, is associated with which indigenous people?
A) Aborigines
B) Sami
C) Native Americans
D) Maori

268. In which country is the traditional art of 'origami' most associated?
A) China
B) Japan
C) South Korea
D) Thailand

269. 'Baguette', a type of long, thin bread, is a culinary icon of which country?
A) Italy
B) France
C) Spain
D) Belgium

270. Which of these languages is considered a Romance language?
A) German
B) Russian
C) Portuguese
D) Hungarian

271. Gumbo, a stew-like dish, is a traditional food in which part of the United States?
A) New England
B) The Midwest
C) The South
D) The Pacific Northwest

272. The Maasai tribe, known for their distinctive customs and dress, is primarily found in which two African countries?
A) Nigeria and Cameroon
B) Kenya and Tanzania
C) South Africa and Namibia
D) Egypt and Sudan

273. Which country is renowned for its ancient tradition of shadow puppetry, known as 'Wayang Kulit'?
A) China
B) Thailand
C) Indonesia
D) India

274. 'Fado' music, characterized by mournful tunes and lyrics, is a genre native to which country?
A) Spain
B) Portugal
C) Brazil
D) Argentina

275. The Inuit, known for their unique cultural practices and adaptation to cold climates, are indigenous to which region?
A) The Amazon Basin
B) Siberia
C) The Arctic
D) The Australian Outback

276. 'Sushi' is a culinary tradition that originated in which country?
    A) China
    B) Vietnam
    C) South Korea
    D) Japan

277. Which city is famous for its historical trade in diamonds and a large orthodox Jewish community?
    A) New York
    B) Mumbai
    C) Tel Aviv
    D) Antwerp

278. 'Holi', the festival of colors, is a significant celebration in which country?
    A) Nepal
    B) Bangladesh
    C) Sri Lanka
    D) India

279. The iconic 'Eiffel Tower' is in which city?
    A) London
    B) Paris
    C) Berlin
    D) Rome

280. The ancient Incan city of Machu Picchu is in which country?
    A) Brazil
    B) Peru
    C) Chile
    D) Argentina

281. 'Reggae' music originated in which country?
    A) Jamaica
    B) Nigeria
    C) Brazil
    D) United States

282. The traditional Russian nesting dolls, known as 'Matryoshka', are a symbol of which culture?
A) Polish
B) Ukrainian
C) Russian
D) Belarusian

283. Which city is famous for its historic canals and gondolas?
A) Amsterdam
B) Venice
C) Copenhagen
D) Bruges

284. 'K-pop', the music genre, originates from which country?
A) China
B) Japan
C) South Korea
D) Thailand

285. Which of these cities is known as 'The City of Light'?
A) New York City
B) Paris
C) London
D) Sydney

286. 'Sauerkraut' is a fermented cabbage dish associated with the cuisine of which country?
A) Poland
B) Germany
C) Russia
D) Austria

287. The ancient pyramids of Giza are in which country?
A) Mexico
B) Sudan
C) Peru
D) Egypt

288. 'Samurai' warriors were part of the feudal history of which country?
A) Japan
B) China
C) Korea
D) Mongolia

289. The 'Louvre Museum', home to the Mona Lisa, is in which city?
A) Rome
B) London
C) Paris
D) Madrid

290. Which country is known for inventing the sport of cricket?
A) Australia
B) India
C) England
D) South Africa

291. The dance form 'Flamenco' is traditionally associated with which country?
A) Mexico
B) Spain
C) Argentina
D) Portugal

292. 'Poutine', a dish featuring fries, cheese curds, and gravy, originated in which country?
A) United States
B) France
C) Canada
D) Belgium

293. The Great Barrier Reef is located off the coast of which country?
A) New Zealand
B) Fiji
C) Australia
D) Indonesia

294. 'Bagpipes' are a traditional musical instrument in the cultural history of which country?
A) Scotland
B) Ireland
C) England
D) Wales

295. 'Carnival of Venice', famous for its elaborate masks, is a historic festival in which country?
A) France
B) Portugal
C) Spain
D) Italy

296. The 'Acropolis', an ancient citadel, is in which city?
A) Rome
B) Athens
C) Istanbul
D) Cairo

297. The traditional attire 'Hanbok' is associated with which country?
A) China
B) Japan
C) South Korea
D) Vietnam

298. 'Salsa' music and dance style is most associated with which culture?
A) Mexican
B) Brazilian
C) Cuban
D) Colombian

299. The 'Oktoberfest' festival, famous for its beer and festivities, originated in which country?
A) Austria
B) Belgium
C) Switzerland
D) Germany

300. Which country is known for its traditional 'Samba' music and dance?
A) Argentina
B) Brazil
C) Colombia
D) Mexico

301. 'Manga' is a style of comic book or graphic novel originating from which country?
A) South Korea
B) China
C) Japan
D) Thailand

302. 'Dim Sum' is a style of Chinese cuisine prepared as small bite-sized portions. In which part of China did it originate?
A) Sichuan
B) Guangdong (Canton)
C) Beijing
D) Shanghai

303. Which country is renowned for its historic 'Viking' culture?
A) Germany
B) Denmark
C) Norway
D) Iceland

304. 'Ceviche', a seafood dish, is particularly associated with the cuisine of which country?
A) Mexico
B) Peru
C) Spain
D) Portugal

305. 'Tango', a dance and music genre, originated in which two countries?
A) Brazil and Portugal
B) Spain and Italy
C) Argentina and Uruguay
D) Colombia and Venezuela

Section 6: Population & Demographics

306. What is the term for the movement of people from rural to urban areas?
A) Urbanization
B) Migration
C) Emigration
D) Immigration

307. Which continent has the highest population density?
A) Asia
B) Europe
C) Africa
D) North America

308. What does a population pyramid represent?
A) Economic status of a country
B) Age and sex distribution of a population
C) Population density of urban areas
D) Migration patterns

309. Which of the following is a primary factor in population growth?
A) Urbanization
B) Industrialization
C) Technological advancement
D) Fertility rate

310. What term describes the number of people living per unit area of land?
A) Population density
B) Population distribution
C) Carrying capacity
D) Demographic scale

311. Which country is known for implementing a one-child policy to control population growth?
A) India
B) China
C) Japan
D) Brazil

312. The term "brain drain" refers to:
A) Decrease in skilled labor due to migration
B) Increase in educational facilities in urban areas
C) Decline in agricultural practices
D) Increase in technological advancements

313. What is the estimated population of China?
A) 1.3 billion
B) 1.4 billion
C) 1.5 billion
D) 1.6 billion

314. Which of the following countries is the most populous?
A) India
B) United States
C) Indonesia
D) Brazil

315. Which European country has a population exceeding 80 million?
A) France
B) Germany
C) Spain
D) Italy

316. Which African country has a population over 200 million?
A) South Africa
B) Egypt
C) Nigeria
D) Ethiopia

317. What is the estimated population of Canada?
A) 25 million
B) 37 million
C) 45 million
D) 50 million

318. Which of these countries has the smallest population?
A) Australia
B) Portugal
C) Malaysia
D) Finland

319. Which country has a population closest to 50 million?
A) South Korea
B) Colombia
C) Kenya
D) Spain

320. Which South American country has a population exceeding 210 million?
A) Argentina
B) Chile
C) Brazil
D) Peru

321. Which city in India is estimated to have a population surpassing 20 million?
A) Delhi
B) Mumbai
C) Bangalore
D) Kolkata

322. What is the population range of London, UK?
A) 4-6 million
B) 6-8 million
C) 8-10 million
D) 10-12 million

323. Which region in the world has the highest population density?
A) East Asia
B) South Asia
C) Southeast Asia
D) Western Europe

324. What is the estimated population of the African continent?
A) 800 million
B) 1 billion
C) 1.2 billion
D) 1.4 billion

325. Which Australian city has a population closest to 5 million?
A) Sydney
B) Melbourne
C) Brisbane
D) Perth

326. Which South American city has a population exceeding 10 million?
A) Buenos Aires, Argentina
B) Rio de Janeiro, Brazil
C) São Paulo, Brazil
D) Bogotá, Colombia

327. Which is the most populous city in the United States?
A) New York City
B) Los Angeles
C) Chicago
D) Houston

328. What is the estimated population of the European Union?
A) 400 million
B) 450 million
C) 500 million
D) 550 million

329. Which of the following cities is the most populous in Africa?
A) Lagos, Nigeria
B) Cairo, Egypt
C) Johannesburg, South Africa
D) Nairobi, Kenya

330. What is the estimated population of the Middle East region?
A) 200 million
B) 250 million
C) 300 million
D) 350 million

331. Which country is expected to surpass China in population by 2030?
A) United States
B) India
C) Indonesia
D) Brazil

332. Which country has a larger population?
A) Mexico
B) Japan
C) Germany
D) Nigeria

333. What is the estimated population of Southeast Asia?
A) 500 million
B) 650 million
C) 700 million
D) 800 million

334. Which country in South America has the smallest population?
A) Uruguay
B) Paraguay
C) Ecuador
D) Suriname

335. What is the estimated population of the Caribbean islands?
A) 20 million
B) 30 million
C) 40 million
D) 50 million

336. Which of these countries has the youngest median age?
A) Canada
B) Nigeria
C) Japan
D) Italy

337. Which continent is projected to have the largest population increase by 2050?
A) Asia
B) Africa
C) Europe
D) South America

338. Which country has a higher population density?
A) Australia
B) India
C) Canada
D) Russia

339. Which Asian country has the most rapidly aging population?
A) South Korea
B) China
C) Thailand
D) India

340. Which region has the highest urban population proportion?
A) North America
B) Europe
C) Asia
D) Africa

341. What is the estimated global population?
A) 7 billion
B) 7.5 billion
C) 8 billion
D) 8.5 billion

342. Which country has the highest life expectancy?
A) Japan
B) Switzerland
C) Australia
D) Monaco

343. Which country has the most significant population decline in Europe?
A) Italy
B) Germany
C) Bulgaria
D) Ukraine

344. What is the estimated global urbanization rate?
A) 45%
B) 55%
C) 65%
D) 75%

345. Which country has experienced the most significant population growth due to immigration?
A) Canada
B) Germany
C) United Arab Emirates
D) Australia

346. Which South American country has the highest literacy rate?
A) Brazil
B) Argentina
C) Chile
D) Uruguay

347. What percentage of the world's population lives in Asia?
A) About 30%
B) About 40%
C) About 50%
D) About 60%

348. Which African country has the highest population growth rate?
A) Nigeria
B) Ethiopia
C) Egypt
D) DR Congo

349. Which country has a higher median age?
A) United States
B) Brazil
C) India
D) Sweden

350. What is the estimated population of the Arctic region?
A) Less than 1 million
B) 1-2 million
C) 2-3 million
D) 3-4 million

351. Which city has the largest expatriate population?
A) Dubai
B) New York City
C) London
D) Singapore

Section 7: Languages & Religion Of The World

352. What is the official language of Brazil?
A) Spanish
B) Quechua
C) Brazilian
D) Portuguese

353. Which language is written from right to left and is the official language of Israel?
A) Arabic
B) Hebrew
C) Yiddish
D) Farsi

354. What is the most widely spoken language in the world by the number of native speakers?
A) Spanish
B) English
C) Mandarin Chinese
D) Hindi

355. In which country is the language Swahili predominantly spoken?
A) Nigeria
B) Kenya
C) South Africa
D) Egypt

356. Which language family does English belong to?
A) Romance
B) Slavic
C) Germanic
D) Celtic

357. Which of the following languages uses the Cyrillic script?
A) Russian
B) Greek
C) Arabic
D) Hindi

358. What is the language spoken by the majority of Switzerland?
A) German
B) French
C) Italian
D) Swiss

359. Which of these languages is a tonal language, where the tone of a word can change its meaning?
A) French
B) Italian
C) Mandarin Chinese
D) German

360. Which language is known for having the most extensive vowel system, with over 20 vowel sounds?
A) Spanish
B) Finnish
C) Zulu
D) Arabic

361. In which country is Punjabi one of the official languages?
A) India
B) Pakistan
C) Bangladesh
D) Sri Lanka

362. What is the official language of Iran?
A) Turkish
B) Farsi
C) Urdu
D) Pashto

363. Which language is the most widely spoken native language in South America?
A) Portuguese
B) Guarani
C) Quechua
D) Spanish

364. In which African country is Afrikaans commonly spoken?
A) Nigeria
B) South Africa
C) Kenya
D) Morocco

365. What is the official language of Egypt?
A) Arabic
B) Persian
C) Turkish
D) Greek

366. Which language is primarily spoken in the Philippines?
A) English
B) Spanish
C) Tagalog
D) Vietnamese

367. Which language is the official language of Argentina?
A) Portuguese
B) Spanish
C) Italian
D) Quechua

368. In which country is the language Swahili widely spoken as a lingua franca?
A) Ethiopia
B) Tanzania
C) Ghana
D) Madagascar

369. Which language is known for its unique writing system consisting of thousands of characters, such as kanji and hiragana?
A) Korean
B) Chinese
C) Japanese
D) Thai

370. Which language is known for its complex system of gender nouns, with three grammatical genders (masculine, feminine, and neuter)?
A) Russian
B) Hindi
C) German
D) Arabic

371. In which country is the official language a form of Arabic known as "Modern Standard Arabic"?
A) Saudi Arabia
B) Egypt
C) Morocco
D) Iran

372. Which language is the most widely spoken indigenous language in the Americas?
A) Cherokee
B) Navajo
C) Quechua
D) Inuktitut

373. What is the official language of Nigeria, the most populous country in Africa?
A) Arabic
B) Yoruba
C) Hausa
D) English

374. Which language is the most widely spoken indigenous language in Canada?
A) Cree
B) Ojibwe
C) Mohawk
D) Inuktitut

375. In which country is the language Tamil primarily spoken?
A) India
B) Sri Lanka
C) Malaysia
D) Thailand

376. What is the official language of Afghanistan?
A) Urdu
B) Pashto
C) Persian
D) Turkmen

377. Which language is known for its Hangul writing system?
A) Japanese
B) Chinese
C) Korean
D) Thai

378. What is the official language of Ethiopia?
A) Amharic
B) Swahili
C) Tigrinya
D) Oromo

379. Which language is known for its script, Nastalik, and is the official language of Pakistan?
A) Pashto
B) Punjabi
C) Sindhi
D) Urdu

380. What is the official language of Switzerland's canton of Graubünden?
A) German
B) French
C) Italian
D) Romansh

381. Which country has the highest number of native Spanish speakers?
A) Spain
B) Argentina
C) Mexico
D) Colombia

382. Where is the Basque language primarily spoken?
A) Portugal and Spain
B) France and Spain
C) Italy
D) Greece and Turkey

383. In which country is Catalan a co-official language?
A) France
B) Italy
C) Spain
D) Portugal

384. What is the most widely spoken language in India?
A) Hindi
B) Bengali
C) Tamil
D) Marathi

385. Which language is predominantly spoken in Quebec, Canada?
A) English
B) French
C) Spanish
D) Dutch

386. Which language is the most widely spoken indigenous language in Mexico?
A) Nahuatl
B) Mayan
C) Zapotec
D) Mixtec

387. Tagalog is an official language of which country?
A) Thailand
B) Malaysia
C) Philippines
D) Indonesia

388. Which country is home to the largest Arabic-speaking population?
A) Saudi Arabia
B) Egypt
C) Morocco
D) United Arab Emirates

389. Which language is spoken in the Flanders region of Belgium?
A) French
B) German
C) English
D) Dutch

390. What is the predominant religion in India?
A) Christianity
B) Islam
C) Hinduism
D) Buddhism

391. Which country is known as the birthplace of Buddhism?
A) China
B) Japan
C) India
D) Thailand

392. In which country is the Roman Catholic Church the state religion?
A) Italy
B) Vatican City
C) Spain
D) Brazil

393. Shintoism is primarily practiced in which country?
A) China
B) South Korea
C) Japan
D) Vietnam

394. Which country has the highest percentage of Muslims?
A) Saudi Arabia
B) Pakistan
C) Indonesia
D) Iran

395. In which country did Sikhism originate?
A) India
B) Pakistan
C) Afghanistan
D) Bangladesh

396. Taoism is traditionally associated with which country?
A) Japan
B) China
C) South Korea
D) Vietnam

397. Lutheranism is a major branch of Protestant Christianity. Which country is considered its origin?
A) England
B) Germany
C) Sweden
D) Norway

398. Judaism is the historical religion of the Jewish people. Which country has the largest Jewish population?
A) United States
B) Israel
C) Russia
D) France

399. Which country is predominantly Eastern Orthodox Christian?
A) Italy
B) Greece
C) France
D) Spain

400. Zoroastrianism was the state religion of which ancient empire?
A) Roman Empire
B) Egyptian Empire
C) Ottoman Empire
D) Persian Empire

401. Which African country has a significant number of its population practicing Coptic Christianity?
A) Nigeria
B) Kenya
C) Egypt
D) Ethiopia

402. Anglicanism, a form of Christianity, is the official state religion of which country?
A) United States
B) United Kingdom
C) Canada
D) Australia

403. Vajrayana Buddhism is prominent in which country?
A) China
B) Japan
C) Tibet
D) India

404. Which country has the most Rastafarians?
A) Ethiopia
B) Jamaica
C) United States
D) Brazil

405. In which country is the Baha'i Faith believed to have originated?
A) Iran
B) Iraq
C) Israel
D) Egypt

406. Which Scandinavian country is predominantly Lutheran?
A) Denmark
B) Norway
C) Sweden
D) Finland

407. Confucianism has had a significant impact on the culture and history of which country?
A) Japan
B) South Korea
C) China
D) Vietnam

408. Much of the population in Thailand practices which religion?
A) Islam
B) Christianity
C) Hinduism
D) Buddhism

Section 8: Geology & Landforms

409. Which of the following is not a primary type of rock?
A) Igneous
B) Sedimentary
C) Metamorphic
D) Basalt

410. Which of these continents is the largest by land area?
A) Africa
B) Asia
C) Europe
D) North America

411. What type of landform is formed by the movement of tectonic plates?
A) Canyon
B) Mountain
C) Plateau
D) Valley

412. What is the term for a large body of water surrounded by land?
A) Sea
B) Ocean
C) Lake
D) River

413. Which of the following is a primary cause of ocean tides?
A) Wind
B) Sun's heat
C) Moon's gravitational pull
D) Earth's rotation

414. The Ring of Fire is famous for its:
A) Tropical Rainforests
B) Active Volcanoes
C) Extensive Deserts
D) Large River Systems

415. What process describes the movement of continents over time?
A) Erosion
B) Plate Tectonics
C) Photosynthesis
D) Weathering

416. What is the main cause of earthquakes?
A) Lunar cycles
B) Ocean currents
C) Movement of tectonic plates
D) Volcanic activity

417. Which of the following is a greenhouse gas?
A) Oxygen
B) Hydrogen
C) Carbon Dioxide
D) Nitrogen

418. Which layer of Earth is made up of tectonic plates?
A) Crust
B) Mantle
C) Core
D) Lithosphere

419. What is a natural satellite that orbits the Earth?
A) Sun
B) Mars
C) Moon
D) Venus

420. What term describes the point on the Earth's surface directly above the origin of an earthquake?
A) Epicenter
B) Hypocenter
C) Seismic zone
D) Fault line

421. A 'delta' primarily forms at the...
A) Source of a river
B) Confluence of rivers
C) Mouth of a river
D) Mid-point of a river

422. What type of forest is characterized by high rainfall and year-round warmth?
A) Deciduous forest
B) Coniferous forest
C) Temperate forest
D) Rainforest

423. What do glaciers primarily consist of?
A) Liquid water
B) Frozen water
C) Saltwater
D) Water vapor

424. What is the term for a steep, high cliff or face of a rock?
A) Mesa
B) Plateau
C) Escarpment
D) Butte

425. Which gas primarily makes up the Earth's atmosphere?
A) Oxygen
B) Nitrogen
C) Carbon Dioxide
D) Argon

426. Which of the following is a primary factor in the formation of seasons on Earth?
A) Distance from the Sun
B) Earth's rotation
C) Earth's tilt on its axis
D) Moon's orbit

427. What phenomenon occurs when water from the ocean heats up and causes extreme weather conditions?
A) El Niño
B) Gulf Stream
C) Jet Stream
D) Monsoon

428. Which of the following is not a layer of the Earth's atmosphere?
A) Troposphere
B) Stratosphere
C) Lithosphere
D) Mesosphere

429. What is the primary cause of wind?
A) Gravitational forces
B) Earth's rotation
C) Temperature differences
D) Ocean currents

430. A 'fjord' is best described as a...
A) Deep, narrow sea inlet bordered by steep cliffs
B) Large flat area of desert
C) Small island in a river or lake
D) Mountain with a volcanic opening

431. What is the main process that shapes a desert landscape?
A) Volcanism
B) Glaciation
C) Erosion
D) Sedimentation

432. A 'biome' is defined as...
A) A large naturally occurring community of flora and fauna
B) An artificially created ecosystem
C) A specific geographic area with no life
D) A single species of plant or animal

433. What causes the phenomenon of ocean currents?
A) Wind patterns
B) Moon's gravitational pull
C) Earth's magnetic field
D) Marine wildlife movement

434. What term describes an area of land where all of the water under it or draining off of it goes into the same place?
A) Watershed
B) Delta
C) Peninsula
D) Archipelago

435. Which of the following is a characteristic feature of a 'mesa'?
A) A deep, narrow valley
B) A small, flat-topped hill
C) A large, flat-topped hill or mountain
D) A steep, cone-shaped hill

436. What are the lights called that are sometimes visible in the Earth's polar regions?
A) Aurora Borealis and Aurora Australis
B) Solar Flares
C) Lunar Eclipses
D) Star Showers

437. What type of landform is typically characterized by steep sides and a flat top, smaller than a mesa?
A) Plateau
B) Butte
C) Valley
D) Canyon

438. The 'Great Plains' of the United States are an example of which type of landform?
A) Mountain range
B) Plateau
C) Desert
D) Prairie

439. What is the primary process that forms a canyon?
A) Glacial movement
B) Earthquakes
C) River erosion
D) Volcanic eruption

440. Which term describes a narrow strip of land connecting two larger land areas?
A) Peninsula
B) Archipelago
C) Isthmus
D) Delta

441. Atolls are...
A) Ring-shaped coral reefs, islands, or series of islets
B) Steep cliffs by the sea
C) Narrow sea inlets bordered by steep cliffs
D) Large, flat islands

442. A basin is best described as...
A) A flat, low-lying area of land
B) A deep, bowl-shaped landform
C) A mountainous area
D) A long, narrow strip of water

443. Which landform is characterized by a flat, elevated land area with steep slopes on at least one side?
A) Mesa
B) Plateau
C) Butte
D) Terrace

444. Which term describes a large natural stream of water flowing in a channel to the sea, a lake, or another such stream?
A) Ocean
B) Lake
C) River
D) Glacier

445. A gulf is a...
A) Large area of flat land with few trees
B) Deep inlet of the sea almost surrounded by land, with a narrow mouth
C) Mountain with a crater or vent through which lava, rock fragments, hot vapor, and gas erupt
D) Flat-topped mountain with steep sides

446. What type of landform is a reef?
A) A bar of sand or shingle at the mouth of a river
B) A ridge of jagged rock, coral, or sand just above or below the surface of the sea
C) A long, narrow island lying parallel and close to the mainland
D) A steep rock face, especially at the edge of the sea

447. Which landform is a large, continuous area of land that is not significantly interrupted by bodies of water or mountains?
A) Continent
B) Peninsula
C) Island
D) Delta

448. What is a canyon?
A) A large underground cave
B) A deep gorge, typically one with a river flowing through it
C) A high, steep face of rock
D) A shallow valley

449. An 'archipelago' is...
A) A body of water surrounded by land
B) A mountain range within a sea or ocean
C) A group or chain of islands clustered together in a sea or ocean
D) A narrow strip of land with sea on either side

450. Which landform is formed by the action of glaciers?
A) Volcano
B) Fjord
C) Mesa
D) Peninsula

451. A strait is best described as a...
A) Narrow body of water that connects two larger bodies of water
B) Large area of flat land at a high elevation
C) Deep inlet of the sea surrounded by steep cliffs
D) Series of islands formed by coral

452. An isthmus is...
A) A narrow strip of land with sea on either side, forming a link between two larger areas of land
B) A piece of land surrounded by water on all sides
C) A large, unbroken area of wilderness
D) A high, steep face of rock

453. A lagoon is best described as...
A) A shallow body of water separated from a larger body of water by barrier islands or reefs
B) A large area of seawater surrounded by land
C) A narrow passage of water between two larger bodies of water
D) A small, saline lake

454. What is a cape?
A) A high point of land that extends into a river, lake, or ocean
B) A large, flat area of land that is higher than the surrounding land
C) A narrow strip of land connecting two larger landmasses
D) A piece of land that juts out into the sea; a headland

455. Which landform is characterized by a steep, rocky coast rising almost vertically from the ocean?
A) Cliff
B) Delta
C) Plateau
D) Gorge

456. What is an oasis?
A) A fertile spot in a desert where water is found
B) A small island in a river or lake
C) A deep, narrow sea inlet bordered by steep cliffs
D) A large, flat area of land raised above the surrounding land

457. Which term describes a flat, low-lying land built up from soil carried downstream by a river and deposited at its mouth?
A) Delta
B) Peninsula
C) Isthmus
D) Atoll

458. A moraine is...
A) A mountain range
B) A mass of rocks and sediment carried down and deposited by a glacier
C) A deep, narrow valley with steep sides
D) A large, flat area of land with steep sides

459. Which landform is a narrow waterway connecting two larger bodies of water?
A) Strait
B) Gulf
C) Bay
D) Fjord

460. Which rock type is formed by the cooling and solidification of magma or lava?
A) Sedimentary
B) Metamorphic
C) Igneous
D) Hydrothermal

461. What is the most abundant element in the Earth's crust?
A) Iron
B) Oxygen
C) Silicon
D) Aluminum

462. Which type of rock is typically formed through the deposition and solidification of sediment?
A) Igneous
B) Metamorphic
C) Sedimentary
D) Crystalline

463. Granite is an example of which type of rock?
A) Igneous
B) Sedimentary
C) Metamorphic
D) Mineral

464. Slate, a common roofing material, is formed from which type of rock?
A) Igneous
B) Sedimentary
C) Metamorphic
D) Hydrothermal

465. What process turns sediment into sedimentary rock?
A) Melting
B) Erosion
C) Compaction and cementation
D) Crystallization

466. Which rock is formed by the cooling of magma underground?
A) Basalt
B) Pumice
C) Granite
D) Obsidian

467. Marble is a metamorphic form of which rock?
A) Granite
B) Limestone
C) Sandstone
D) Shale

468. Which type of sedimentary rock is primarily composed of mineral calcite?
A) Sandstone
B) Shale
C) Limestone
D) Conglomerate

469. Gneiss is a type of metamorphic rock that has what distinctive feature?
A) Vesicular texture
B) Banding or stripes
C) Glassy surface
D) Fossil content

470. Sandstone is primarily composed of which mineral?
A) Quartz
B) Calcite
C) Feldspar
D) Mica

471. Which type of rock is most likely to contain fossils?
A) Igneous
B) Metamorphic
C) Sedimentary
D) Mineral

472. Obsidian, a natural glass, is an example of what kind of igneous rock?
A) Intrusive
B) Extrusive
C) Metamorphic
D) Sedimentary

473. What is the primary characteristic that distinguishes shale from other sedimentary rocks?
A) Its hardness
B) Its grain size
C) Its color
D) Its layering

474. Which rock is typically formed by the accumulation and consolidation of volcanic ash?
A) Tuff
B) Granite
C) Pumice
D) Basalt

475. What type of rock would you expect to form at the bottom of a deep-sea?
A) Sandstone
B) Shale
C) Limestone
D) Granite

Section 9: Seas & Oceans

476. What percentage of the Earth's surface is covered by oceans?
A) 55%
B) 64%
C) 71%
D) 77%

477. What causes ocean tides?
A) Wind
B) Earth's rotation
C) Gravitational pull of the Moon and Sun
D) Changes in sea level

478. Coral reefs are primarily found in which type of ocean waters?
A) Cold, deep waters
B) Shallow, tropical waters
C) Temperate, coastal waters
D) Deep, tropical waters

479. What is the primary cause of ocean acidification?
A) Overfishing
B) Pollution
C) Increase in sea temperature
D) Absorption of CO_2 from the atmosphere

480. Which of the following gases is most abundant in the ocean?
A) Oxygen
B) Nitrogen
C) Carbon dioxide
D) Argon

481. What is the primary source of oxygen produced in the ocean?
A) Algae
B) Coral reefs
C) Plankton
D) Seaweed

482. Which ocean current is known as the "World's Largest Conveyor Belt"?
A) Gulf Stream
B) Kuroshio Current
C) Antarctic Circumpolar Current
D) Thermohaline Circulation

483. Which phenomenon is characterized by unusually warm ocean temperatures in the Equatorial Pacific?
A) El Niño
B) La Niña
C) Gulf Stream
D) Thermohaline Circulation

484. Which of these is not a layer of the ocean?
A) Epipelagic
B) Mesopelagic
C) Bathypelagic
D) Stratospheric

485. What is the largest sea in the world?
A) Caribbean Sea
B) Coral Sea
C) Philippine Sea
D) Mediterranean Sea

486. Which sea is known for its high salinity?
A) Red Sea
B) Baltic Sea
C) Black Sea
D) Dead Sea

487. The Sargasso Sea is unique because:
A) It has no coastline
B) It is the smallest sea
C) It is completely frozen
D) It is the saltiest sea

488. What process describes the movement of salt and nutrients from the deep sea to the surface?
A) Desalination
B) Upwelling
C) Evaporation
D) Condensation

489. Which sea separates the Italian and Balkan peninsulas?
A) Adriatic Sea
B) Aegean Sea
C) Ionian Sea
D) Tyrrhenian Sea

490. The Great Barrier Reef is located in which sea?
A) Coral Sea
B) Tasman Sea
C) Arafura Sea
D) Timor Sea

491. Which sea is an extension of the Indian Ocean?
A) Arabian Sea
B) Red Sea
C) Baltic Sea
D) Mediterranean Sea

492. What is the deepest point in the Mediterranean Sea?
A) Calypso Deep
B) Mariana Trench
C) Puerto Rico Trench
D) Java Trench

493. The Sea of Galilee is primarily located in which country?
A) Jordan
B) Israel
C) Egypt
D) Syria

494. Which sea is known for the phenomenon of the Midnight Sun?
A) Baltic Sea
B) Barents Sea
C) Black Sea
D) Caspian Sea

495. The Caspian Sea is unique because:
A) It's the smallest sea
B) It's the deepest sea
C) It's the saltiest sea
D) It's the world's largest lake

496. Which sea is famous for the legend of the Bermuda Triangle?
A) Red Sea
B) North Sea
C) Adriatic Sea
D) Caribbean Sea

497. The Sea of Japan is bordered by all the following countries except:
A) China
B) Russia
C) North Korea
D) South Korea

498. Which sea is the largest inland sea?
A) Aral Sea
B) Caspian Sea
C) Dead Sea
D) Salton Sea

499. The Sea of Marmara joins which two larger bodies of water?
A) Aegean Sea and Mediterranean Sea
B) Black Sea and Caspian Sea
C) Mediterranean Sea and Black Sea
D) Adriatic Sea and Aegean Sea

500. Which sea is known for its historically significant trade routes?
A) Mediterranean Sea
B) Baltic Sea
C) Arabian Sea
D) South China Sea

501. The Hudson Bay, often considered a sea, is part of which country?
A) United States
B) Canada
C) Russia
D) Greenland

502. Which sea is the smallest in the world?
A) Baltic Sea
B) Sea of Azov
C) Black Sea
D) Adriatic Sea

503. The Bering Sea is located between which two countries?
A) United States and Canada
B) Russia and Japan
C) United States and Russia
D) Canada and Russia

504. Which sea is known for the mysterious disappearance of ships and airplanes?
A) North Sea
B) Baltic Sea
C) Caribbean Sea
D) Sargasso Sea

505. The Tyrrhenian Sea is part of which larger body of water?
A) Atlantic Ocean
B) Mediterranean Sea
C) Indian Ocean
D) Pacific Ocean

506. Which sea is directly north of the Aegean Sea?
A) Black Sea
B) Adriatic Sea
C) Mediterranean Sea
D) Ionian Sea

507. The Yellow Sea is located between which two countries?
A) Japan and Russia
B) China and South Korea
C) North Korea and South Korea
D) China and Japan

508. Which sea is famous for its 'Sea of Stars' phenomenon, caused by bioluminescent plankton?
A) Caribbean Sea
B) Sea of Okhotsk
C) Arabian Sea
D) Indian Ocean

509. The Andaman Sea is part of which ocean?
A) Indian Ocean
B) Pacific Ocean
C) Atlantic Ocean
D) Arctic Ocean

510. The Sea of Tranquility, famously named in the context of space exploration, is found on:
A) Mars
B) The Moon
C) Jupiter
D) Saturn

511. Which sea is known for the historical Viking explorations?
A) Mediterranean Sea
B) Baltic Sea
C) North Sea
D) Adriatic Sea

512. The Persian Gulf is an extension of which sea?
A) Arabian Sea
B) Red Sea
C) Mediterranean Sea
D) Caspian Sea

513. The Sea of Crete is part of which larger sea?
A) Aegean Sea
B) Mediterranean Sea
C) Ionian Sea
D) Adriatic Sea

514. The Weddell Sea is located near which continent?
A) Africa
B) Australia
C) Antarctica
D) South America

515. Which sea is known for the Battle of Lepanto, a significant naval engagement in history?
A) Adriatic Sea
B) Mediterranean Sea
C) Aegean Sea
D) Ionian Sea

516. The Gulf of Guinea is part of which ocean?
A) Atlantic Ocean
B) Indian Ocean
C) Pacific Ocean
D) Southern Ocean

517. Which sea is known for the historical city of Troy on its shores?
A) Black Sea
B) Aegean Sea
C) Mediterranean Sea
D) Adriatic Sea

518. The Ligurian Sea is located near which European country?
A) Spain
B) France
C) Italy
D) Greece

519. What is the primary inlet of the Baltic Sea?
A) Kattegat
B) Gulf of Bothnia
C) Skagerrak
D) Strait of Gibraltar

520. Which ocean is known as the warmest?
A) Southern Ocean
B) Pacific Ocean
C) Atlantic Ocean
D) Indian Ocean

521. Which ocean surrounds the continent of Antarctica?
A) Southern Ocean
B) Arctic Ocean
C) Atlantic Ocean
D) Indian Ocean

522. The Sargasso Sea is in which ocean?
A) Southern Ocean
B) Pacific Ocean
C) Indian Ocean
D) Atlantic Ocean

523. The Great Barrier Reef, the world's largest coral reef system, is in which ocean?
A) Atlantic Ocean
B) Pacific Ocean
C) Indian Ocean
D) Southern Ocean

524. Which ocean is the smallest and shallowest?
A) Arctic Ocean
B) Southern Ocean
C) Indian Ocean
D) Atlantic Ocean

525. The Bermuda Triangle is in which ocean?
A) Indian Ocean
B) Pacific Ocean
C) Atlantic Ocean
D) Arctic Ocean

526. The Ring of Fire is mostly located in which ocean?
A) Indian Ocean
B) Atlantic Ocean
C) Pacific Ocean
D) Arctic Ocean

527. The Mozambique Channel lies in which ocean?
A) Southern Ocean
B) Atlantic Ocean
C) Pacific Ocean
D) Indian Ocean

528. Which ocean is the second largest in the world?
A) Atlantic Ocean
B) Southern Ocean
C) Indian Ocean
D) Pacific Ocean

529. The Ninety East Ridge is a submarine volcanic ridge located in which ocean?
A) Pacific Ocean
B) Atlantic Ocean
C) Indian Ocean
D) Arctic Ocean

530. Which ocean's name means 'peaceful' in Portuguese?
A) Atlantic Ocean
B) Pacific Ocean
C) Indian Ocean
D) Southern Ocean

531. The Drake Passage connects the Atlantic Ocean with which other ocean?
A) Pacific Ocean
B) Arctic Ocean
C) Indian Ocean
D) Southern Ocean

532. The Gulf Stream is a warm ocean current in which ocean?
A) Pacific Ocean
B) Atlantic Ocean
C) Indian Ocean
D) Southern Ocean

533. Which ocean is home to the island of Madagascar?
A) Indian Ocean
B) Atlantic Ocean
C) Pacific Ocean
D) Southern Ocean

534. The Humboldt Current is associated with which ocean?
A) Indian Ocean
B) Atlantic Ocean
C) Pacific Ocean
D) Southern Ocean

535. Which sea is known for containing the island of Komodo, famous for its dragons?
A) Coral Sea
B) Java Sea
C) Timor Sea
D) Arafura Sea

536. The Laptev Sea is part of which ocean?
A) Arctic Ocean
B) Atlantic Ocean
C) Pacific Ocean
D) Indian Ocean

537. The Sea of Azov is connected to which larger sea?
A) Red Sea
B) Caspian Sea
C) Mediterranean Sea
D) Black Sea

538. The Tasman Sea is located between Australia and which other country?
A) Indonesia
B) New Zealand
C) Papua New Guinea
D) Fiji

539. Which sea is bordered by the Sinai Peninsula to the west?
A) Red Sea
B) Mediterranean Sea
C) Black Sea
D) Arabian Sea

540. The Bay of Bengal is an extension of which ocean?
A) Indian Ocean
B) Pacific Ocean
C) Atlantic Ocean
D) Arctic Ocean

541. Which sea is known as the birthplace of ancient Greek mythology's Jason and the Argonauts?
A) Aegean Sea
B) Black Sea
C) Ionian Sea
D) Mediterranean Sea

542. The Labrador Sea is part of which ocean?
A) Indian Ocean
B) Pacific Ocean
C) Arctic Ocean
D) Atlantic Ocean

543. Which sea is located between Vietnam and the Philippines?
A) Celebes Sea
B) East China Sea
C) South China Sea
D) Sulu Sea

544. The Alboran Sea is the westernmost part of which larger sea?
A) Mediterranean Sea
B) Black Sea
C) Red Sea
D) Aegean Sea

545. Which sea is famous for the sinking of the RMS Titanic?
A) North Sea
B) Norwegian Sea
C) Baltic Sea
D) North Atlantic Ocean

546. The Cook Strait separates the North and South islands of which country?
A) Australia
B) New Zealand
C) Indonesia
D) Papua New Guinea

547. Which sea is known for the unique wildlife of the Galapagos Islands?
A) Caribbean Sea
B) Coral Sea
C) Pacific Ocean
D) South China Sea

548. The Gulf of Aden connects which two bodies of water?
A) Arabian Sea and Red Sea
B) Mediterranean Sea and Red Sea
C) Indian Ocean and Red Sea
D) Arabian Sea and Persian Gulf

549. The Sea of Okhotsk is part of which ocean?
A) Pacific Ocean
B) Arctic Ocean
C) Atlantic Ocean
D) Indian Ocean

550. Which sea is known for the historic maritime city of Venice?
A) Adriatic Sea
B) Mediterranean Sea
C) Aegean Sea
D) Ionian Sea

551. The Strait of Malacca is a crucial shipping lane in which sea?
A) Andaman Sea
B) South China Sea
C) Java Sea
D) Timor Sea

Section 10: Countries, Borders & Regions

552. Which of these countries is landlocked?
A) Brazil
B) Ethiopia
C) Mexico
D) Japan

553. Which continent has the greatest number of countries?
A) Africa
B) Europe
C) Asia
D) North America

554. Which country is known for having a city that spans two continents?
A) Egypt
B) Russia
C) Turkey
D) Kazakhstan

555. In which country is the Great Wall located?
A) Japan
B) China
C) Mongolia
D) South Korea

556. Which country is surrounded by South Africa?
A) Namibia
B) Botswana
C) Eswatini
D) Lesotho

557. Which of the following countries is not a member of the European Union?
A) Sweden
B) Norway
C) Poland
D) Italy

558. Which country is the most populous in Africa?
A) South Africa
B) Egypt
C) Nigeria
D) Ethiopia

559. Which of these countries is not a permanent member of the United Nations Security Council?
A) United States
B) Russia
C) Germany
D) China

560. Which country is famous for its fjords?
A) Finland
B) Norway
C) Iceland
D) Sweden

561. Which of these countries is not part of the United Kingdom?
A) Scotland
B) Wales
C) Ireland
D) England

562. Which is the most densely populated country in the world?
A) Monaco
B) Singapore
C) Vatican City
D) Bangladesh

563. Which country is known as the Land of the Rising Sun?
A) Japan
B) South Korea
C) China
D) Thailand

564. Which country does Greenland belong to?
A) Norway
B) Canada
C) Iceland
D) Denmark

565. Which country has the largest population in the world?
A) India
B) United States
C) Indonesia
D) China

566. Which of these countries is not a member of the North Atlantic Treaty Organization (NATO)?
A) France
B) Turkey
C) Switzerland
D) United Kingdom

567. Which country is known for its unique shape resembling a boot?
A) Portugal
B) Italy
C) Croatia
D) Spain

568. Which is the smallest country in South America by land area?
A) Uruguay
B) Paraguay
C) Ecuador
D) Suriname

569. Which country is divided into 50 states?
A) Canada
B) Mexico
C) United States
D) Brazil

570. Which country is famous for the region of Transylvania?
A) Hungary
B) Slovakia
C) Bulgaria
D) Romania

571. Which country does the island of Sicily belong to?
A) Greece
B) Italy
C) Spain
D) France

572. Which country is known as the "Land Down Under"?
A) New Zealand
B) South Africa
C) Australia
D) Argentina

573. Which two countries share the longest international border in the world?
A) United States and Mexico
B) Russia and China
C) Canada and United States
D) Russia and Kazakhstan

574. Which country is bordered by both the Atlantic and Indian Oceans?
A) Australia
B) South Africa
C) Russia
D) India

575. What is the only country that borders the United Kingdom?
A) France
B) Netherlands
C) Belgium
D) Ireland

576. Which two countries share the greatest number of international borders?
A) China and Russia
B) Germany and France
C) Brazil and Argentina
D) India and Pakistan

577. What natural barrier forms part of the border between the United States and Canada?
A) Rocky Mountains
B) Great Lakes
C) Mississippi River
D) Grand Canyon

578. Which two countries are separated by the Pyrenees Mountains?
A) France and Spain
B) Switzerland and Italy
C) Germany and Austria
D) Norway and Sweden

579. Which country shares a border with the most neighbors?
A) Russia
B) China
C) Brazil
D) Germany

580. Which two African countries are separated by the Victoria Falls?
A) Zambia and Zimbabwe
B) Kenya and Tanzania
C) South Africa and Namibia
D) Egypt and Sudan

581. The DMZ (Demilitarized Zone) separates which two countries?
A) North Korea and South Korea
B) India and Pakistan
C) Germany East and West (historically)
D) China and Mongolia

582. What is the only country that borders Monaco?
A) Italy
B) Spain
C) France
D) Switzerland

583. Which two countries share the Iguazu Falls?
A) Brazil and Argentina
B) Venezuela and Colombia
C) Bolivia and Peru
D) Paraguay and Uruguay

584. Which European country is bordered by nine other countries, the most in Europe?
A) Germany
B) France
C) Ukraine
D) Serbia

585. What body of water separates Saudi Arabia from Africa?
A) Mediterranean Sea
B) Red Sea
C) Persian Gulf
D) Gulf of Aden

586. Which two countries are separated by the Strait of Gibraltar?
A) Portugal and Spain
B) Tunisia and Italy
C) Spain and the United Kingdom
D) Spain and Morocco

587. Mount Everest forms part of the border between which two countries?
A) India and China
B) Nepal and China
C) Bhutan and India
D) Nepal and India

588. Which country has coastlines on both the Caribbean Sea and the Pacific Ocean?
A) Mexico
B) Colombia
C) Panama
D) Nicaragua

589. The Mekong River forms a part of the border for which country?
A) Vietnam
B) Thailand
C) Laos
D) Cambodia

590. What strait separates Tasmania from the mainland of Australia?
A) Torres Strait
B) Bass Strait
C) Cook Strait
D) Arafura Sea

591. Which two countries are divided by the Bering Strait?
    A) United States and Russia
    B) Canada and Greenland
    C) Russia and Japan
    D) Norway and Russia

592. What river forms a significant part of the border between India and Bangladesh?
    A) Ganges
    B) Brahmaputra
    C) Indus
    D) Yamuna

593. Which two countries share the longest border in Africa?
    A) Algeria and Libya
    B) Democratic Republic of the Congo and Angola
    C) Sudan and South Sudan
    D) Egypt and Sudan

594. Which two countries are separated by the English Channel?
    A) France and Spain
    B) United Kingdom and Ireland
    C) France and United Kingdom
    D) Belgium and United Kingdom

595. The Amur River forms part of the border between Russia and which other country?
    A) Mongolia
    B) Kazakhstan
    C) China
    D) North Korea

596. What is the primary political subdivision of the United States?
    A) Counties
    B) States
    C) Regions
    D) Provinces

597. Which two countries share the world's highest international border?
A) India and Nepal
B) Pakistan and China
C) India and China
D) Nepal and China

598. What separates Morocco from the Spanish territories of Ceuta and Melilla?
A) Mediterranean Sea
B) Atlas Mountains
C) Sahara Desert
D) Fences and fortifications

599. What natural barrier forms the Argentina / Chile border?
A) Pampas
B) Amazon Rainforest
C) Andes Mountains
D) Patagonia Desert

600. In which country are 'cantons' a key political subdivision?
A) France
B) Switzerland
C) Germany
D) Italy

601. What are the political subdivisions of Canada called?
A) States
B) Provinces and Territories
C) Departments
D) Regions

602. In India, the main political subdivisions are known as?
A) States and Union Territories
B) Provinces
C) Prefectures
D) Regions

603. Prefectures are a form of political subdivision in which country?
A) China
B) Japan
C) South Korea
D) Vietnam

604. In Russia, the largest political subdivisions are known as?
A) Oblasts
B) Republics
C) Regions
D) Federal Districts

605. What are the political subdivisions in Australia called?
A) States and Territories
B) Counties
C) Provinces
D) Departments

606. In the United Kingdom, which is not a political subdivision?
A) Counties
B) Parishes
C) Boroughs
D) States

607. Departments are used as political subdivisions in which of these countries?
A) Spain
B) France
C) Italy
D) Greece

608. What is the capital of the Catalonia region in Spain?
A) Madrid
B) Barcelona
C) Seville
D) Valencia

609. Which region in Italy is known for its leaning tower?
A) Tuscany
B) Lombardy
C) Veneto
D) Sicily

610. The 'Black Forest' is a famous wooded mountain range in which German region?
A) Bavaria
B) Baden-Württemberg
C) Saxony
D) Hesse

611. Which region in France is famous for its wine production?
A) Normandy
B) Brittany
C) Provence
D) Bordeaux

612. The Silicon Valley, known for its technology industry, is in which U.S. state?
A) California
B) Texas
C) New York
D) Florida

613. The Great Barrier Reef is located off the coast of which Australian state?
A) New South Wales
B) Queensland
C) Victoria
D) Western Australia

614. Which region in the UK is known for its distinctive dialect and industrial heritage?
A) Cornwall
B) Yorkshire
C) Surrey
D) Kent

615. 'Punjab' is a region in India and which other country?
A) Nepal
B) Pakistan
C) Bangladesh
D) Bhutan

616. The Sahara Desert covers a large part of which region in Africa?
A) West Africa
B) Central Africa
C) North Africa
D) Southern Africa

617. What is the capital of Alberta, a province in Canada?
A) Calgary
B) Edmonton
C) Vancouver
D) Toronto

618. Which Russian region is known for being the coldest inhabited place on Earth?
A) Siberia
B) Kamchatka
C) Ural
D) Volga

619. The Amazon Rainforest is primarily located in which Brazilian region?
A) Southeast
B) South
C) Northeast
D) North

620. Which region in China is known for its terracotta army?
A) Guangdong
B) Shaanxi
C) Yunnan
D) Sichuan

621. Mount Fuji is in which region of Japan?
A) Kanto
B) Chubu
C) Kansai
D) Tohoku

622. The Maasai Mara National Reserve is a large game reserve in which region of Kenya?
A) Rift Valley
B) Central
C) Nyanza
D) Eastern

623. Which region in Italy is known for its capital, Naples, and the historic ruins of Pompeii?
A) Campania
B) Lazio
C) Sicily
D) Lombardy

624. The Andalusia region, known for flamenco music and dance, is in which country?
A) Portugal
B) Spain
C) Italy
D) Greece

625. Patagonia is a region located in the southern part of which two countries?
A) Chile and Argentina
B) Bolivia and Peru
C) Brazil and Uruguay
D) Colombia and Venezuela

626. The Loire Valley, famous for its castles and vineyards, is in which French region?
A) Normandy
B) Île-de-France
C) Centre-Val de Loire
D) Brittany

627. Which region in the United States is known for its large Amish population?
A) New England
B) Midwest
C) Pacific Northwest
D) Pennsylvania Dutch Country

628. The Basque Country, known for its unique culture and language, is in which country?
A) Spain
B) France
C) Italy
D) Portugal

629. The Ruhr area, a major industrial region, is in which country?
A) France
B) Germany
C) Belgium
D) Netherlands

630. The Scottish Highlands are part of which UK country?
A) Scotland
B) England
C) Wales
D) Northern Ireland

631. The Napa Valley, famous for its wineries, is in which U.S. state?
A) Arizona
B) Oregon
C) Washington
D) California

632. The Kimberley, known for its dramatic landscapes, is a region in which Australian state?
A) Victoria
B) Queensland
C) New South Wales
D) Western Australia

633. The Kruger National Park, a major wildlife reserve, is in which South African province?
A) Gauteng
B) Limpopo
C) Western Cape
D) KwaZulu-Natal

634. The Algarve region is in which country?
A) Spain
B) Portugal
C) Italy
D) Greece

635. Lombardy, a region with Milan as its capital, is in which country?
A) France
B) Spain
C) Italy
D) Germany

636. Which region in the United States is known for its large technology industry, including Silicon Valley?
A) The Midwest
B) The Northeast
C) The Pacific Northwest
D) The West Coast

637. Sicily, an island region, is part of which country?
A) Italy
B) Greece
C) Spain
D) France

638. Which region in India is known for its tea plantations and Himalayan views?
A) Kerala
B) Rajasthan
C) West Bengal
D) Assam

639. The Galapagos Islands are a province of which country?
A) Colombia
B) Ecuador
C) Peru
D) Chile

640. Normandy, a region known for its WWII beaches, is located in which country?
A) United Kingdom
B) France
C) Belgium
D) Netherlands

641. Transylvania, associated with the legend of Dracula, is a region in which country?
A) Romania
B) Hungary
C) Bulgaria
D) Slovakia

642. The Okavango Delta, a unique inland delta, is in which region of Botswana?
A) North-East District
B) South-East District
C) North-West District
D) Central District

643. Cappadocia, known for its unique landscapes and cave dwellings, is in which country?
A) Greece
B) Turkey
C) Italy
D) Spain

644. The Lake District, a popular area for hiking and boating, is in which UK country?
A) Scotland
B) England
C) Wales
D) Northern Ireland

645. Which Mexican state is famous for the city of Cancun?
A) Baja California
B) Yucatán
C) Jalisco
D) Quintana Roo

646. What is the largest province by area in Canada?
A) British Columbia
B) Alberta
C) Ontario
D) Quebec

647. In which U.S. state is the Grand Canyon located?
A) Arizona
B) Colorado
C) Nevada
D) New Mexico

648. Which is the only Canadian province that is officially bilingual (English and French)?
A) Quebec
B) Ontario
C) New Brunswick
D) Manitoba

649. The ancient Mayan city of Chichen Itza is located in which Mexican state?
A) Chiapas
B) Yucatán
C) Tabasco
D) Quintana Roo

650. Which U.S. state is known as the 'Sunshine State'?
A) California
B) Florida
C) Hawaii
D) Texas

651. What is the smallest province by area in Canada?
A) Prince Edward Island
B) Nova Scotia
C) New Brunswick
D) Newfoundland and Labrador

652. Which U.S. state is known as the 'Land of 10,000 Lakes'?
A) Minnesota
B) Michigan
C) Wisconsin
D) Alaska

653. The city of Vancouver is in which Canadian province?
A) British Columbia
B) Alberta
C) Ontario
D) Quebec

654. Which Canadian province is the largest producer of maple syrup?
A) Quebec
B) Ontario
C) Nova Scotia
D) New Brunswick

655. Which U.S. state is known for the city of Las Vegas?
A) Nevada
B) California
C) Arizona
D) New Mexico

656. Baarle-Hertog, a complicated mix of Belgian enclaves, is in which country's territory primarily?
A) Belgium
B) Netherlands
C) Luxembourg
D) France

657. Which two countries are separated by the Diomede Islands, where one island belongs to each country, and they are only about 4 km apart?
A) Canada and Greenland
B) Russia and Japan
C) United States and Russia
D) Norway and Sweden

658. Which two African countries have a nearly straight-line vertical border that runs for about 2,159 km (1,341 miles), one of the longest straight borders in the world?
A) Egypt and Sudan
B) Libya and Chad
C) Algeria and Mali
D) Namibia and Angola

659. Where is the only place in the world where four countries meet at a single point?
A) Botswana, Zambia, Zimbabwe, and Namibia
B) India, Bhutan, China, and Nepal
C) Brazil, Peru, Colombia, and Venezuela
D) Afghanistan, Pakistan, China, and Tajikistan

660. Pheasant Island on the Bidasoa river is a unique condominium. It alternates sovereignty between France and which other country?
A) Belgium
B) Switzerland
C) Spain
D) Italy

661. Where can you find the town of Llívia, a Spanish exclave entirely surrounded by France?
A) Along the French Riviera
B) Near the Mediterranean coast
C) In the Pyrenees
D) In the Alps

662. The Penon de Velez de la Gomera, one of the world's shortest land borders (about 85 meters), is between Spain and which country?
A) Morocco
B) Algeria
C) Gibraltar (UK)
D) Portugal

663. Campione d'Italia is an Italian exclave surrounded by which country?
A) France
B) Austria
C) Slovenia
D) Switzerland

664. The Wagah Border, famous for its elaborate border ceremonies, is between which two countries?
A) China and Mongolia
B) North Korea and South Korea
C) India and Pakistan
D) Germany and Poland

665. The Northwest Angle is part of the United States but is only accessible by land through which country?
A) Canada
B) Mexico
C) Russia
D) Greenland

666. Hans Island is a disputed territory between which two countries?
A) Norway and Russia
B) Canada and Denmark
C) United States and Canada
D) Russia and United States

Section 11: Islands

667. Which island is known as the "Island of the Gods"?
A) Bali
B) Sicily
C) Crete
D) Maui

668. What is the largest island in the world?
A) Greenland
B) New Guinea
C) Borneo
D) Australia

669. Which island is famous for its Moai statues?
A) Fiji
B) Easter Island
C) Galapagos Islands
D) Tahiti

670. Which island is the birthplace of Napoleon Bonaparte?
A) Corsica
B) Sardinia
C) Sicily
D) Elba

671. What is the largest island in the Mediterranean Sea?
A) Cyprus
B) Crete
C) Sicily
D) Sardinia

672. Which island is famously known for the Komodo dragon?
A) Sumatra
B) Borneo
C) Java
D) Komodo Island

673. Hawaii's Mauna Kea is a volcano located on which island?
A) Oahu
B) Maui
C) Big Island (Hawaii)
D) Kauai

674. Which island country is known for the legendary city of Atlantis, as described by Plato?
A) Malta
B) Santorini
C) Crete
D) Cyprus

675. Which island in the Caribbean is shared by two countries: the Dominican Republic and Haiti?
A) Jamaica
B) Hispaniola
C) Cuba
D) Puerto Rico

676. Which of these islands is known for its giant tortoises?
A) Madagascar
B) Seychelles
C) Galapagos Islands
D) Fiji

677. The island of Tasmania is a part of which country?
A) New Zealand
B) Australia
C) Indonesia
D) Fiji

678. Which island nation is known as the land of fire and ice?
A) Iceland
B) Greenland
C) Norway
D) Finland

679. Mount Teide is located on which island?
A) Fuerteventura
B) Majorca
C) Tenerife
D) Gran Canaria

680. "The Island of Spice" refers to which Caribbean Island?
A) Grenada
B) Jamaica
C) Barbados
D) Trinidad

681. Which island is known as a major financial center and a British Overseas Territory in the Caribbean?
A) Bermuda
B) Cayman Islands
C) Bahamas
D) Virgin Islands

682. Which Asian island is famous for its orangutans?
A) Java
B) Borneo
C) Sumatra
D) Bali

683. Which island is the principal territory of New Caledonia, a French territory in the Pacific Ocean?
A) Corsica
B) Tahiti
C) Grande Terre
D) Fiji

684. Which Philippine island is famous for its Chocolate Hills?
A) Palawan
B) Luzon
C) Cebu
D) Bohol

685. What is the capital of the Indonesian island of Bali?
A) Ubud
B) Denpasar
C) Kuta
D) Seminyak

686. The island of Zanzibar is part of which African country?
A) Kenya
B) Tanzania
C) Mozambique
D) Madagascar

687. Which is the only US state made up entirely of islands?
A) Florida
B) Rhode Island
C) Puerto Rico
D) Hawaii

688. Which island is known as the "Emerald Isle"?
A) Iceland
B) Ireland
C) Cyprus
D) Jamaica

689. The ancient city of Troy was located on which modern-day Turkish island?
A) Bozcaada
B) Gökçeada
C) None, Troy is on the mainland
D) Marmara Island

690. Which island is famous for the historic naval base of Pearl Harbor?
A) Oahu, Hawaii
B) Maui, Hawaii
C) Midway Island
D) Guam

691. Jeju Island, known for its volcanic landscape and beach resorts, is part of which country?
A) Japan
B) South Korea
C) China
D) Taiwan

692. The island of Sri Lanka is in which ocean?
A) Indian Ocean
B) Pacific Ocean
C) Atlantic Ocean
D) Arctic Ocean

693. Which island is famous for the legendary Loch Ness Monster?
A) Great Britain
B) Ireland
C) Iceland
D) Isle of Man

694. The Galapagos Islands are a part of which country?
A) Ecuador
B) Peru
C) Colombia
D) Chile

695. Which archipelago is known for both its historical significance in World War II and its biodiversity?
A) The Hawaiian Islands
B) The Falkland Islands
C) The Solomon Islands
D) The Aleutian Islands

696. The Maldives are in which ocean?
A) Indian Ocean
B) Pacific Ocean
C) Atlantic Ocean
D) Arctic Ocean

697. Which country does the archipelago of Svalbard belong to?
A) Norway
B) Sweden
C) Russia
D) Canada

698. The Balearic Islands, including Mallorca and Ibiza, are part of which European country?
A) Italy
B) Spain
C) Greece
D) Portugal

699. Which archipelago in the Atlantic Ocean is a British Overseas Territory known for its subtropical climate and pink sand beaches?
A) The Canary Islands
B) The Azores
C) Bermuda
D) The Bahamas

700. The largest island in the Indonesian archipelago is:
A) Sumatra
B) Java
C) Borneo
D) Sulawesi

701. The Aegean Islands are part of which country?
A) Turkey
B) Greece
C) Italy
D) Cyprus

702. Which archipelago includes the islands of Pico, São Miguel, and Terceira?
A) The Azores
B) The Canary Islands
C) The Madeira Islands
D) The Cape Verde Islands

703. The Philippines is composed of approximately how many islands?
A) 500
B) 2,000
C) 5,000
D) 7,600

704. Rapa Nui is a territory of which South American country?
A) Chile
B) Peru
C) Argentina
D) Brazil

705. The Seychelles archipelago is in which ocean?
A) Indian Ocean
B) Atlantic Ocean
C) Pacific Ocean
D) Southern Ocean

706. Which archipelago is famous for the historic city of Venice?
A) The Balearic Islands
B) The Cyclades
C) The Venetian Lagoon
D) The Dalmatian Islands

707. The Shetland Islands are part of which country?
A) Norway
B) Scotland
C) Iceland
D) Denmark

708. The Faroe Islands are a self-governing archipelago under the sovereignty of which country?
A) Iceland
B) Norway
C) Denmark
D) United Kingdom

709. Which Caribbean archipelago is a commonwealth of the United States?
A) The Virgin Islands
B) The Bahamas
C) The Cayman Islands
D) Puerto Rico

710. The archipelago of Tierra del Fuego is shared by which two South American countries?
A) Argentina and Chile
B) Brazil and Uruguay
C) Peru and Ecuador
D) Colombia and Venezuela

711. The Cape Verde archipelago is located off the coast of which continent?
A) South America
B) Africa
C) Europe
D) North America

712. The Cook Islands are in free association with which country?
A) Australia
B) France
C) United States
D) New Zealand

713. The archipelago of Zanzibar is part of which African country?
A) Kenya
B) Tanzania
C) Mozambique
D) Madagascar

714. The Thousand Islands archipelago is located along the border of the United States and which other country?
A) Canada
B) Mexico
C) Russia
D) Iceland

715. The Okinawa Islands are part of which country?
A) China
B) Taiwan
C) South Korea
D) Japan

716. The Andaman and Nicobar Islands are a territory of which country?
A) Indonesia
B) India
C) Thailand
D) Malaysia

717. Which archipelago is known as the "Land of Fire"?
A) The Aleutian Islands
B) The Canary Islands
C) Tierra del Fuego
D) The Hebrides

718. The Outer Hebrides belong to which country?
A) Ireland
B) Norway
C) Scotland
D) Iceland

719. The Kuril Islands are disputed between Russia and which other country?
A) China
B) Japan
C) South Korea
D) United States

720. The island of Corsica is a territorial collectivity of which country?
A) Italy
B) Spain
C) France
D) Greece

721. The Lofoten Islands are located in which country?
A) Finland
B) Norway
C) Sweden
D) Denmark

722. The Pitcairn Islands are the last British Overseas Territory in which ocean?
A) Indian Ocean
B) Pacific Ocean
C) Atlantic Ocean
D) Arctic Ocean

723. The Spratly Islands are a region of territorial disputes involving multiple countries in which sea?
A) South China Sea
B) East China Sea
C) Java Sea
D) Philippine Sea

Section 12: Cities, Buildings & Landmarks

724. Which monument is in the center of Red Square in Moscow?
A) The Kremlin
B) Saint Basil's Cathedral
C) The Hermitage Museum
D) The Bolshoi Theatre

725. In which city can you visit the Acropolis?
A) Rome
B) Athens
C) Istanbul
D) Cairo

726. Where is the Statue of Liberty located?
A) San Francisco
B) Boston
C) New York City
D) Washington D.C.

727. Where is the Taj Mahal located?
A) Delhi
B) Mumbai
C) Agra
D) Kolkata

728. Which city is known for the Colosseum?
A) Athens
B) Paris
C) Rome
D) Madrid

729. Which city is home to the Burj Khalifa skyscraper?
A) Dubai
B) Riyadh
C) Doha
D) Abu Dhabi

730. Which city is famous for the Golden Gate Bridge?
A) Los Angeles
B) San Francisco
C) New York City
D) Seattle

731. Where can you find the ancient ruins of Petra?
A) Egypt
B) Israel
C) Jordan
D) Saudi Arabia

732. The famous Buckingham Palace is located in which city?
A) London
B) Oxford
C) Buckingham
D) Cambridge

733. Mount Rushmore, featuring the carved faces of four U.S. presidents, is in which state?
A) California
B) South Dakota
C) Montana
D) Wyoming

734. Which city is known for the iconic structure known as the "Bean" (Cloud Gate)?
A) New York City
B) Chicago
C) Los Angeles
D) San Francisco

735. Where is the historic site Stonehenge located?
A) Ireland
B) Scotland
C) England
D) Wales

736. The Temple of the Emerald Buddha is a famous landmark in which city?
A) Hanoi
B) Kuala Lumpur
C) Jakarta
D) Bangkok

737. Which city is known as the "City of Light"?
A) New York City
B) London
C) Jerusalem
D) Paris

738. The Great Pyramid of Giza is located in which country?
A) Jordan
B) Saudi Arabia
C) Egypt
D) Morocco

739. Which city is home to the iconic landmark, the Kremlin?
A) St. Petersburg
B) Warsaw
C) Kiev
D) Moscow

740. In which city can you find the historic site, Alcatraz Island?
A) Los Angeles
B) San Francisco
C) Seattle
D) San Diego

741. The famous 'Leaning Tower' is located in which Italian city?
A) Rome
B) Venice
C) Florence
D) Pisa

742. Where is the historic Angkor Wat temple complex located?
A) Thailand
B) Cambodia
C) Vietnam
D) Laos

743. Which city is famous for its vibrant nightlife and is often called the "City that Never Sleeps"?
A) Las Vegas
B) New York City
C) Tokyo
D) Paris

744. The Rialto Bridge is a famous landmark in which city?
A) Amsterdam
B) Venice
C) Paris
D) London

745. Which city is known for the iconic Times Square?
A) Los Angeles
B) Chicago
C) New York City
D) Miami

746. The Hermitage Museum is located in which city?
A) Moscow
B) Berlin
C) St. Petersburg
D) Paris

747. Which city is famous for the historic landmark, the Tower Bridge?
A) London
B) New York City
C) Sydney
D) Paris

748. In which city can you visit the Van Gogh Museum?
A) Amsterdam
B) Paris
C) Berlin
D) London

749. The famous 'Christ the Redeemer' statue overlooks which city?
A) Buenos Aires
B) Rio de Janeiro
C) Santiago
D) São Paulo

750. In which city is the iconic 'Gateway Arch' located?
A) Chicago
B) New York City
C) St. Louis
D) San Francisco

751. The Guggenheim Museum, known for its unique architecture, is in which city?
A) Los Angeles
B) Chicago
C) New York City
D) San Francisco

752. Which city is home to the historic site, the Alhambra?
A) Madrid
B) Seville
C) Granada
D) Barcelona

753. In which city is the famous 'Notre-Dame Cathedral' located?
A) London
B) Madrid
C) Rome
D) Paris

754. Where can you find the ancient temple complex known as 'The Parthenon'?
A) Rome
B) Cairo
C) Istanbul
D) Athens

755. Which city is famous for hosting the Summer Olympics in 2000?
A) Beijing
B) Rio de Janeiro
C) London
D) Sydney

756. The famous 'Blue Mosque' is located in which city?
A) Cairo
B) Istanbul
C) Tehran
D) Baghdad

757. In which city is the 'Prado Museum' located?
A) Barcelona
B) Madrid
C) Seville
D) Lisbon

758. Which city is known for the historic 'Forbidden City'?
A) Beijing
B) Shanghai
C) Tokyo
D) Seoul

759. Château de Versailles is a palace located near which city?
A) Paris
B) Strasbourg
C) Marseille
D) Bordeaux

760. The 'Victoria Falls' is located on the border of which two African countries?
A) Kenya and Tanzania
B) Ethiopia and Eritrea
C) South Africa and Namibia
D) Zambia and Zimbabwe

761. Which city is known for its 'Art Deco Historic District'?
A) New York City
B) Miami
C) Los Angeles
D) San Francisco

762. The 'Anne Frank House' is in which city?
A) Berlin
B) Paris
C) Warsaw
D) Amsterdam

763. The 'Temple of Heaven' is a historical landmark in which city?
A) Beijing
B) Shanghai
C) Tokyo
D) Seoul

764. Which city is famous for the historic 'Wailing Wall'?
A) Cairo
B) Istanbul
C) Jerusalem
D) Tehran

765. Which city is known for the iconic landmark, the Space Needle?
A) Chicago
B) Seattle
C) Toronto
D) New York City

766. The historic site 'Mont Saint-Michel' is in which country?
A) Italy
B) Spain
C) France
D) Portugal

767. Which city is famous for the landmark 'Big Ben'?
A) Paris
B) London
C) Berlin
D) Madrid

768. In which city is the Uffizi Gallery, one of the oldest art museums in the world, located?
A) Rome
B) Milan
C) Florence
D) Venice

769. In which city can you visit the historic 'Hagia Sophia'?
A) Istanbul
B) Jerusalem
C) Athens
D) Cairo

770. Which city is home to the historic 'Liberty Bell'?
A) Boston
B) New York City
C) Philadelphia
D) Washington D.C.

771. The 'Cliffs of Moher' are in which country?
A) Scotland
B) Ireland
C) England
D) Wales

772. Where can you find the historical landmark 'The Pantheon'?
A) Athens
B) Rome
C) Paris
D) London

773. Which city is known for the 'Akihabara' district, famous for its electronics and anime culture?
A) Beijing
B) Seoul
C) Tokyo
D) Shanghai

774. The 'Neuschwanstein Castle', which inspired Disney's Sleeping Beauty Castle, is in which country?
A) Austria
B) Germany
C) Switzerland
D) France

775. In which city is the famous 'Copacabana Beach' located?
A) Buenos Aires
B) Santiago
C) Rio de Janeiro
D) Lima

776. Which city is famous for the 'Nyhavn' harbor, known for its brightly colored townhouses and boats?
A) Amsterdam
B) Copenhagen
C) Stockholm
D) Oslo

777. The 'Terracotta Army' is a famous archaeological site in which country?
A) Japan
B) South Korea
C) China
D) Vietnam

778. In which city can you find the 'Guggenheim Museum', known for its unique architecture?
A) Madrid
B) Barcelona
C) Bilbao
D) Seville

779. What is the name of the famous clock tower located at the north end of the Palace of Westminster in London?
A) The Elizabeth Tower
B) Big Ben
C) The Victoria Tower
D) The Westminster Clock

780. The 'Petronas Towers', once the tallest buildings in the world, are located in which city?
A) Bangkok
B) Jakarta
C) Singapore
D) Kuala Lumpur

781. Which building is known as the 'house of the president' of the United States?
A) Capitol Building
B) White House
C) Pentagon
D) Lincoln Memorial

782. The Lotus Temple, notable for its flowerlike shape, is in which city?
A) Mumbai
B) Chennai
C) Bangalore
D) Delhi

783. In which city is the 'Shard', the tallest building in the UK, located?
A) Manchester
B) Birmingham
C) London
D) Edinburgh

784. The 'Taipei 101' skyscraper is located in which city?
A) Beijing
B) Shanghai
C) Hong Kong
D) Taipei

785. The 'Willis Tower' (formerly Sears Tower), once the tallest building in the world, is located in which city?
A) New York City
B) Chicago
C) Los Angeles
D) San Francisco

786. The 'One World Trade Center', also known as the 'Freedom Tower', is located in which city?
A) Washington D.C.
B) Boston
C) New York City
D) Philadelphia

787. In which city is the 'Sagrada Família', a large unfinished Roman Catholic church, located?
A) Madrid
B) Lisbon
C) Rome
D) Barcelona

788. Which city is known for the 'CCTV Headquarters', famous for its distinctive looped shape?
A) Tokyo
B) Seoul
C) Beijing
D) Shanghai

789. The 'Chrysler Building', a classic example of Art Deco architecture, is located in which city?
A) Chicago
B) Detroit
C) New York City
D) Los Angeles

790. The 'CN Tower', once the world's tallest free-standing structure, is located in which city?
A) Toronto
B) Vancouver
C) Montreal
D) Ottawa

791. Which building is known for its historic significance as a former royal palace and prison in France?
A) Palace of Versailles
B) Louvre Museum
C) Notre-Dame de Paris
D) Bastille

792. The 'Flatiron Building', known for its unique triangular shape, is located in which city?
A) New York City
B) Chicago
C) San Francisco
D) Los Angeles

793. In which city is the 'Fallingwater' house, designed by Frank Lloyd Wright, located?
A) Chicago
B) New York
C) Los Angeles
D) Mill Run, Pennsylvania

794. The 'Atomium', a building designed to resemble the structure of an atom, is located in which city?
A) Paris
B) Brussels
C) Amsterdam
D) Berlin

795. Which city is home to the 'Marina Bay Sands', known for its unique architecture and rooftop infinity pool?
A) Singapore
B) Kuala Lumpur
C) Bangkok
D) Hong Kong

796. In which city can you find the 'J. Edgar Hoover Building', the main office of the FBI?
A) New York City
B) Los Angeles
C) Chicago
D) Washington D.C.

797. The 'Lloyds Building', known for its futuristic design, is located in which city?
A) New York
B) London
C) Tokyo
D) Dubai

798. Which city is known for the 'Belem Tower', a historic tower located at the mouth of the Tagus River?
A) Lisbon
B) Porto
C) Barcelona
D) Madrid

799. The 'Palace of Parliament', known as one of the largest administrative buildings in the world, is located in which city?
A) Moscow
B) Bucharest
C) Prague
D) Budapest

800. In which city is the 'Kingdom Centre', a skyscraper with a distinctive hole near its top, located?
A) Dubai
B) Riyadh
C) Doha
D) Abu Dhabi

801. The 'Bank of China Tower', known for its prism-like structure, is located in which city?
A) Beijing
B) Shanghai
C) Hong Kong
D) Taipei

802. Which city is home to the '30 St Mary Axe', commonly known as 'The Gherkin' due to its shape?
A) London
B) New York City
C) Sydney
D) Toronto

803. The 'Turning Torso', a neo-futurist residential skyscraper, is located in which city?
A) Copenhagen
B) Stockholm
C) Malmö
D) Oslo

804. In which city is the 'Gateway of India', an arch-monument built during the 20th century, located?
A) New Delhi
B) Kolkata
C) Bangalore
D) Mumbai

805. The 'Reichstag Building', home to the German parliament, is located in which city?
A) Berlin
B) Munich
C) Frankfurt
D) Hamburg

806. Which city is famous for the 'Oriental Pearl Tower', known for its unique architectural design?
A) Beijing
B) Shanghai
C) Hong Kong
D) Guangzhou

Section 13: Extreme Weather & Natural Disasters

807. What is the primary cause of a hurricane?
A) Tectonic plate movement
B) Air pollution
C) Solar flares
D) Oceanic temperature rise

808. Which scale is used to measure the intensity of tornadoes?
A) Richter Scale
B) Fujita Scale
C) Saffir-Simpson Scale
D) Beaufort Scale

809. What is the term for a prolonged period of abnormally low rainfall?
A) Drought
B) Heatwave
C) Blizzard
D) Tsunami

810. Which of these is a secondary effect of earthquakes?
A) Tsunamis
B) Lightning
C) Tornadoes
D) Hailstorms

811. What is the main difference between a hurricane and a typhoon?
A) Size and intensity
B) Name based on location
C) Season of occurrence
D) Wind speed

812. What causes a tsunami?
A) High winds
B) Rapid snowmelt
C) Heavy rainfall
D) Underwater volcanic eruption or earthquake

813. What is an ice storm?
A) Heavy snowfall with strong winds
B) A storm with freezing rain
C) A cold wave with low temperatures
D) A blizzard over an ocean

814. Which layer of the atmosphere do most tornadoes form in?
A) Troposphere
B) Stratosphere
C) Mesosphere
D) Thermosphere

815. What is the main difference between a cyclone and a tornado?
A) Size
B) Location of formation
C) Wind speed
D) Duration

816. What phenomenon is often responsible for causing El Niño?
A) Volcanic activity
B) Solar radiation
C) Oceanic temperature variations
D) Deforestation

817. What causes most avalanches?
A) Earthquakes
B) Volcanic eruptions
C) Heavy snowfall
D) High winds

818. In what area do most earthquakes occur?
A) Along oceanic ridges
B) In desert regions
C) In polar regions
D) Along tectonic plate boundaries

819. What is the main cause of landslides?
A) Deforestation
B) Urban development
C) Volcanic eruptions
D) Earthquakes or heavy rain

820. Which gas is most released during a volcanic eruption?
A) Oxygen
B) Ammonia
C) Carbon dioxide
D) Sulfur

821. What is the Beaufort Scale used to measure?
A) Earthquake intensity
B) Wind speed
C) Ocean wave height
D) Rainfall intensity

822. What type of natural disaster is typically associated with a pyroclastic flow?
A) Earthquake
B) Tsunami
C) Volcanic eruption
D) Tornado

823. What causes a dust storm?
A) Heavy rainfall
B) Strong winds in arid or semi-arid regions
C) Oceanic temperature rise
D) Tectonic plate movements

824. Which of these is not a sign of an impending volcanic eruption?
A) Earthquakes
B) Sudden drop in temperature
C) Formation of new lakes
D) Change in water temperature

825. What is a mudflow?
A) Slow movement of earth due to gravity
B) Rapid flow of mud due to water saturation
C) Formation of cracks in dry land
D) Movement of sand dunes

826. What is the main cause of thunderstorms?
A) Cold fronts
B) Low humidity
C) High-pressure systems
D) Warm, moist air rising and cooling

827. What is the term for the boundary where two different air masses meet?
A) Convergence zone
B) Pressure ridge
C) Jet stream
D) Front

828. What is commonly used to categorize the severity of a hurricane?
A) Fujita Scale
B) Richter Scale
C) Saffir-Simpson Hurricane Wind Scale
D) Beaufort Scale

829. Which natural disaster is primarily caused by the movement of the Earth's tectonic plates?
A) Floods
B) Earthquakes
C) Hurricanes
D) Wildfires

830. What is the primary cause of a tsunami?
A) Heavy rainfall
B) Melting glaciers
C) Underwater earthquakes or volcanic eruptions
D) Strong winds

831. Which of the following best describes a lahar?
A) A dry landslide
B) A volcanic mudflow
C) A high-speed avalanche
D) A type of hurricane

832. What type of cloud is commonly associated with thunderstorms?
A) Cirrus
B) Stratus
C) Cumulus
D) Cumulonimbus

833. Which of these is not a type of avalanche?
A) Powder snow avalanche
B) Wet snow avalanche
C) Rock avalanche
D) Mud avalanche

834. What is the primary cause of sinkholes?
A) Tectonic plate movements
B) Oceanic temperature rise
C) Natural weathering of limestone
D) Volcanic eruptions

835. What hurricane hit New Orleans in August 2005, causing widespread destruction and flooding?
A) Hurricane Katrina
B) Hurricane Sandy
C) Hurricane Maria
D) Hurricane Irma

836. In 2010, which country experienced a devastating earthquake, leading to significant humanitarian efforts?
A) Japan
B) Haiti
C) Indonesia
D) Nepal

837. The 2004 Indian Ocean tsunami was triggered by an earthquake in which region?
A) Andaman Islands
B) Sumatra, Indonesia
C) Sri Lanka
D) Thailand

838. Which European country experienced a deadly heatwave in the summer of 2003?
A) Germany
B) Spain
C) France
D) Italy

839. In 1980, the eruption of Mount St. Helens occurred in which U.S. state?
A) Washington
B) Oregon
C) California
D) Alaska

840. The Dust Bowl of the 1930s severely affected which part of the United States?
A) Northeast
B) Southeast
C) Midwest
D) Great Plains

841. What year did Hurricane Sandy, also known as Superstorm Sandy, strike the East Coast of the United States?
A) 2012
B) 2010
C) 2013
D) 2011

842. The Great Flood of 1993 occurred along which American river?
A) Mississippi River
B) Missouri River
C) Colorado River
D) Ohio River

843. Which Asian country experienced a catastrophic tsunami in 2011, followed by a nuclear disaster?
A) China
B) Japan
C) Thailand
D) Indonesia

844. What year was the Black Saturday bushfires that ravaged parts of Victoria, Australia?
A) 2009
B) 2010
C) 2008
D) 2007

845. Typhoon Haiyan, one of the strongest tropical cyclones ever recorded, hit which country in 2013?
A) Philippines
B) Vietnam
C) China
D) Malaysia

846. The Great Galveston Hurricane, the deadliest in U.S. history, occurred in what year?
A) 1900
B) 1910
C) 1920
D) 1899

847. In 1953, a catastrophic North Sea flood affected the Netherlands and which other country significantly?
A) Germany
B) Denmark
C) Belgium
D) United Kingdom

848. The Loma Prieta earthquake of 1989 affected which U.S. city the most?
A) Los Angeles
B) San Diego
C) Seattle
D) San Francisco

849. In 2005, Hurricane Wilma became the most intense Atlantic hurricane on record in terms of:
A) Wind speed
B) Barometric pressure
C) Size
D) Duration

850. The 1991 eruption of Mount Pinatubo occurred in which country?
A) Japan
B) Philippines
C) Indonesia
D) Thailand

851. Which country was hit by Cyclone Nargis in 2008, one of the deadliest cyclones in history?
A) India
B) Bangladesh
C) Myanmar
D) Sri Lanka

852. The Tri-State Tornado of 1925 affected which three U.S. states?
A) Indiana, Ohio, and Kentucky
B) Missouri, Illinois, and Indiana
C) Kansas, Missouri, and Oklahoma
D) Illinois, Indiana, and Ohio

853. In which year did the Great Lisbon Earthquake, accompanied by a tsunami and fire, occur?
A) 1755
B) 1800
C) 1850
D) 1700

854. The deadliest blizzard in history occurred in 1972 in which country?
A) Canada
B) United States
C) Iran
D) Russia

855. Which island nation was severely impacted by Hurricane Mitch in 1998?
A) Cuba
B) Haiti
C) Honduras
D) Jamaica

856. The 1931 China floods, considered one of the deadliest natural disasters in history, primarily occurred along which river?
A) Yellow River
B) Yangtze River
C) Pearl River
D) Mekong River

857. In 2003, which country experienced its most destructive wildfire, known as the Canberra Bushfires?
A) New Zealand
B) Australia
C) South Africa
D) United States

858. The 1999 Odisha Cyclone, one of the strongest recorded tropical cyclones in the North Indian Ocean, hit which country?
A) Bangladesh
B) Sri Lanka
C) Myanmar
D) India

859. In what year did the Great Hanshin Earthquake, also known as the Kobe Earthquake, occur in Japan?
A) 1995
B) 1990
C) 2000
D) 1985

860. The 1985 Nevado del Ruiz volcano eruption, triggering a deadly mudslide, took place in which country?
A) Mexico
B) Colombia
C) Chile
D) Peru

861. Which African country experienced severe droughts leading to a famine in 1984-1985?
A) Nigeria
B) Somalia
C) Ethiopia
D) Sudan

862. The Ash Wednesday Bushfires of 1983 occurred in which two Australian states?
A) New South Wales and Queensland
B) South Australia and Queensland
C) Western Australia and Tasmania
D) Victoria and South Australia

863. In 2005, Tropical Storm Stan caused severe damage and landslides in Central America, particularly affecting which country?
A) Guatemala
B) El Salvador
C) Nicaragua
D) Costa Rica

864. What year did the Tangshan Earthquake, one of the deadliest in the 20th century, occur in China?
A) 1976
B) 1968
C) 1980
D) 1972

Section 14: Deserts

865. Which desert is famous for its unique red sand?
A) Kalahari Desert
B) Namib Desert
C) Atacama Desert
D) Simpson Desert

866. What causes the formation of deserts?
A) High rainfall
B) Ocean currents
C) Wind patterns and geographical location
D) Dense vegetation

867. Which desert has the Saguaro cactus?
A) Mojave Desert
B) Great Victoria Desert
C) Chihuahuan Desert
D) Sonoran Desert

868. The Sahara Desert is primarily located in which continent?
A) Asia
B) Africa
C) South America
D) Australia

869. What is a primary adaptation of animals living in the desert?
A) Long fur
B) Webbed feet
C) Water conservation
D) Cold resistance

870. What is the primary vegetation found in deserts?
A) Large trees
B) Grasslands
C) Shrubs and cacti
D) Dense forests

871. Which desert is known for the 'Valley of the Moon'?
A) Atacama Desert
B) Sonoran Desert
C) Gobi Desert
D) Thar Desert

872. The Gobi Desert is primarily located in which two countries?
A) China and Mongolia
B) India and Pakistan
C) United States and Mexico
D) Egypt and Sudan

873. What is the main feature of a desert ecosystem?
A) High humidity
B) Abundant water sources
C) Scarcity of water
D) Dense forest cover

874. Which desert is known for the unique geological formations called 'The Wave'?
A) Kalahari Desert
B) Great Basin Desert
C) Sahara Desert
D) Mojave Desert

875. In which continent is the Thar Desert located?
A) Africa
B) Asia
C) Australia
D) North America

876. What phenomenon often causes mirages in deserts?
A) Earthquakes
B) Refraction of light
C) Heavy rainfall
D) Sandstorms

877. Which desert is the hottest in the world?
A) Kalahari Desert
B) Gobi Desert
C) Atacama Desert
D) Lut Desert

878. What adaptation helps cacti to survive in desert conditions?
A) Bright flowers
B) Deep roots
C) Thick, water-storing stems
D) Poisonous spines

879. The 'Desert of Forbidden Art' is a documentary about an art collection hidden in which desert?
A) Sahara Desert
B) Karakum Desert
C) Sonoran Desert
D) Gobi Desert

880. Which desert has a famous salt flat known as 'Salar de Uyuni'?
A) Atacama Desert
B) Great Victoria Desert
C) Mojave Desert
D) Sahara Desert

881. Deserts typically receive less than how many inches of rainfall per year?
A) 50 inches
B) 25 inches
C) 10 inches
D) 5 inches

882. Which South American desert is known for its high altitude?
A) Atacama Desert
B) Patagonian Desert
C) Sechura Desert
D) Monte Desert

883. The Great Victoria Desert is located in which country?
A) South Africa
B) United States
C) Australia
D) Mexico

884. What is the primary source of moisture in the Namib Desert?
A) River floods
B) Underground springs
C) Fog and dew
D) Rainfall

885. Desert plants like cacti often have spines instead of leaves primarily to:
A) Attract pollinators
B) Reduce water loss
C) Capture prey
D) Provide shade

886. Which desert is known for its large dune fields, such as Rub' al Khali or the Empty Quarter?
A) Sonoran Desert
B) Kalahari Desert
C) Gobi Desert
D) Arabian Desert

887. The Chihuahuan Desert is located in which two countries?
A) Australia and New Zealand
B) Argentina and Chile
C) Egypt and Sudan
D) United States and Mexico

888. What is the main reason for the formation of oasis in deserts?
A) Meteor showers
B) Underground water sources
C) Animal activity
D) Wind patterns

889. The Mojave Desert is known for a unique tree species called:
A) Baobab
B) Redwood
C) Joshua Tree
D) Sequoia

890. Which desert is known for the Death Valley, the lowest point in North America?
A) Mojave Desert
B) Sonoran Desert
C) Great Basin Desert
D) Chihuahuan Desert

891. Which desert is primarily located in China and Mongolia?
A) Gobi Desert
B) Thar Desert
C) Kalahari Desert
D) Arabian Desert

892. What type of desert is formed on the leeward side of a mountain range due to the rain shadow effect?
A) Coastal Desert
B) Rainforest Desert
C) Mountain Desert
D) Polar Desert

893. The famous Uluru (Ayers Rock) is in which desert of Australia?
A) Simpson Desert
B) Great Victoria Desert
C) Gibson Desert
D) Great Sandy Desert

894. Which desert is known for the historic Silk Road trade route?
A) Sahara Desert
B) Gobi Desert
C) Kalahari Desert
D) Sonoran Desert

895. What unique feature is observed in the White Desert of Egypt?
A) Large salt flats
B) Unusually shaped chalk rock formations
C) The world's deepest cave
D) Rare desert waterfalls

896. The unique phenomenon of 'Singing Sands' can be experienced in which desert?
A) Namib Desert
B) Sahara Desert
C) Atacama Desert
D) Gobi Desert

897. Which desert is known for its diverse range of flora and fauna, including the kangaroo rat and the creosote bush?
A) Sahara Desert
B) Mojave Desert
C) Kalahari Desert
D) Arabian Desert

898. What is the primary factor that determines a desert's location on Earth?
A) Proximity to oceans
B) Altitude
C) Latitude
D) Rainfall patterns

Section 15: Geography World Records

899. What is the largest country in the world by area?
A) China
B) Russia
C) Canada
D) United States

900. Which country has the longest coastline in the world?
A) Australia
B) Canada
C) Russia
D) Indonesia

901. Where is the deepest point in the world's oceans located?
A) Mariana Trench
B) Tonga Trench
C) Philippine Trench
D) Java Trench

902. What is the world's smallest country by land area?
A) Monaco
B) Nauru
C) Vatican City
D) San Marino

903. Which river is the longest in the world?
A) Amazon
B) Nile
C) Yangtze
D) Mississippi

904. What is the world's largest desert?
A) Arabian Desert
B) Sahara Desert
C) Gobi Desert
D) Antarctic Desert

905. Which is the highest mountain peak in the world?
A) K2
B) Kangchenjunga
C) Lhotse
D) Mount Everest

906. What is the largest ocean in the world?
A) Atlantic Ocean
B) Indian Ocean
C) Pacific Ocean
D) Southern Ocean

907. Which lake is the deepest in the world?
A) Lake Baikal
B) Tanganyika
C) Caspian Sea
D) Crater Lake

908. Which country is known as the land of a thousand lakes?
A) Finland
B) Canada
C) Sweden
D) Norway

909. What is the largest island in the world?
A) Greenland
B) New Guinea
C) Borneo
D) Madagascar

910. Which country has the most volcanoes?
A) Japan
B) Indonesia
C) United States
D) Italy

911. What is the longest river in Asia?
A) Indus River
B) Mekong River
C) Ganges River
D) Yangtze River

912. Which country is the most populous in the world?
A) India
B) United States
C) China
D) Indonesia

913. Where is the lowest land point on Earth's surface?
A) Turpan Depression
B) Lake Assal
C) Death Valley
D) Dead Sea

914. What is the driest place on Earth?
A) McMurdo, Antarctica
B) Sahara Desert
C) Kufra, Libya
D) Atacama Desert

915. Which mountain range is the longest in the world?
A) The Andes
B) The Rockies
C) The Himalayas
D) The Alps

916. Which is the largest coral reef system in the world?
A) Belize Barrier Reef
B) Red Sea Coral Reef
C) Great Barrier Reef
D) New Caledonia Barrier Reef

917. What is the most densely populated country in the world?
A) Monaco
B) Singapore
C) Vatican City
D) Bangladesh

918. Which country is known for having the most natural lakes?
A) Finland
B) Canada
C) Russia
D) United States

919. What is the highest active volcano in the world?
A) Mount Kilimanjaro
B) Mount Etna
C) Cotopaxi
D) Ojos del Salado

920. Which is the smallest ocean in the world?
A) Arctic Ocean
B) Indian Ocean
C) Atlantic Ocean
D) Southern Ocean

921. What is the largest gulf in the world?
A) Gulf of Mexico
B) Persian Gulf
C) Gulf of Guinea
D) Gulf of Alaska

922. Which country has the most UNESCO World Heritage Sites?
A) Italy
B) China
C) France
D) Spain

923. What is the most earthquake-prone country in the world?
A) Indonesia
B) Japan
C) Chile
D) Nepal

924. Which continent is the driest on Earth?
A) Asia
B) Africa
C) Australia
D) Antarctica

925. What country has the longest river system in North America?
A) Canada
B) United States
C) Mexico
D) Guatemala

926. Which city is the highest capital in the world?
A) Quito, Ecuador
B) La Paz, Bolivia
C) Kathmandu, Nepal
D) Thimphu, Bhutan

927. What is the largest lake in Africa?
A) Lake Malawi
B) Lake Tanganyika
C) Lake Victoria
D) Lake Chad

928. What is the longest mountain range underwater?
A) Marianas Trench
B) East Pacific Rise
C) Mid-Atlantic Ridge
D) Arctic Mid-Ocean Ridge

929. Which is the largest delta in the world?
A) Ganges-Brahmaputra Delta
B) Mississippi Delta
C) Nile Delta
D) Mekong Delta

930. What is the most populous city in the world?
A) Tokyo, Japan
B) Delhi, India
C) Shanghai, China
D) Sao Paulo, Brazil

931. Which country has the most time zones?
A) Russia
B) United States
C) Canada
D) France

932. What is the oldest active volcano on Earth?
A) Mount Vesuvius
B) Mount Etna
C) Mauna Loa
D) Eyjafjallajökull

933. What is the largest tropical rainforest in the world?
A) Congo Rainforest
B) Amazon Rainforest
C) Daintree Rainforest
D) Southeast Asian Rainforest

934. Which river has the greatest discharge at its mouth?
A) Amazon River
B) Congo River
C) Yangtze River
D) Ganges River

935. What is the highest waterfall in the world?
A) Niagara Falls
B) Victoria Falls
C) Angel Falls
D) Tugela Falls

936. Which is the largest archipelago in the world by area?
A) Maldives
B) Philippines
C) Indonesia
D) Japan

937. Which is the hottest continent on Earth?
A) Africa
B) Australia
C) South America
D) Asia

938. What is the longest river in Europe?
A) Danube
B) Volga
C) Ural
D) Rhine

939. Which country has the most islands in the world?
A) Philippines
B) Indonesia
C) Finland
D) Sweden

940. What is the largest peninsula in the world?
A) Arabian Peninsula
B) Indian Peninsula
C) Scandinavian Peninsula
D) Iberian Peninsula

941. What is the highest plateau in the world?
A) Bolivian Plateau
B) Deosai National Park, Pakistan
C) Tibetan Plateau
D) Colorado Plateau, USA

942. Which is the largest bay in the world?
A) Bay of Bengal
B) Hudson Bay
C) Bay of Biscay
D) Chesapeake Bay

943. What country has the longest continuous coastline on a single landmass?
A) Australia
B) Canada
C) Russia
D) Norway

944. Which country has the highest number of lakes in the world?
A) Canada
B) Finland
C) Russia
D) United States

945. What is the largest salt flat in the world?
A) Bonneville Salt Flats, USA
B) Salar de Uyuni, Bolivia
C) Makgadikgadi Pan, Botswana
D) Salinas Grandes, Argentina

Section 16: Historical Countries & Cities

946. Which city is known as the 'Cradle of Renaissance'?
A) Paris
B) Rome
C) Florence
D) Athens

947. The Great Wall of China was primarily built to protect against invasions from which group?
A) The Huns
B) The Mongols
C) The Japanese
D) The Tibetans

948. Which ancient city is associated with the Trojan War?
A) Athens
B) Sparta
C) Troy
D) Rome

949. The city of Tenochtitlan, founded in 1325, is the predecessor of which modern-day city?
A) Lima
B) Mexico City
C) Buenos Aires
D) Havana

950. The city of Constantinople, a pivotal city in history, is known today as:
A) Athens
B) Jerusalem
C) Cairo
D) Istanbul

951. Which city was the capital of the British Empire at its peak?
A) New York
B) London
C) Toronto
D) Sydney

952. Timbuktu, an important city in the history of West Africa, is in which modern-day country?
A) Mali
B) Nigeria
C) Ghana
D) Senegal

953. Which city was the center of the Aztec civilization?
A) Chichen Itza
B) Cuzco
C) Teotihuacan
D) Tenochtitlan

954. The historical city of Petra, known for its rock-cut architecture, is in which country?
A) Egypt
B) Jordan
C) Israel
D) Saudi Arabia

955. Which ancient civilization built the city of Carthage?
A) Romans
B) Greeks
C) Phoenicians
D) Egyptians

956. Which city was the first capital of the United States?
A) New York City
B) Philadelphia
C) Washington D.C.
D) Boston

957. The Meiji Restoration, which transformed Japan into a modern state, began in what year?
A) 1905
B) 1853
C) 1898
D) 1868

958. What was the original name of New York City when it was a Dutch colony?
A) New Amsterdam
B) New Netherland
C) New Utrecht
D) New Holland

959. Which empire was centered around the city of Cusco?
A) Inca Empire
B) Aztec Empire
C) Maya Civilization
D) Olmec Civilization

960. The ancient city of Babylon was located in what is now:
A) Egypt
B) Iraq
C) Iran
D) Syria

961. The ancient city of Sparta was located in which country?
A) Italy
B) Egypt
C) Greece
D) Turkey

962. What was the capital of the Ottoman Empire?
A) Cairo
B) Baghdad
C) Istanbul
D) Damascus

963. Which city was the capital of the ancient kingdom of Siam, now known as Thailand?
A) Chiang Mai
B) Ayutthaya
C) Bangkok
D) Sukhothai

964. The city of Leningrad, renamed in 1991, is known today as:
A) Moscow
B) Sochi
C) Vladivostok
D) St. Petersburg

965. Which city was the birthplace of the Industrial Revolution?
A) London
B) Manchester
C) Liverpool
D) Birmingham

966. Varanasi, one of the oldest inhabited cities, is where?
A) Nepal
B) India
C) Bangladesh
D) Pakistan

967. The Kingdom of Prussia existed until what year?
A) 1871
B) 1918
C) 1945
D) 1989

968. The ancient city of Persepolis was the ceremonial capital of which empire?
A) Roman Empire
B) Egyptian Empire
C) Macedonian Empire
D) Persian Empire

969. The city of Pompeii was part of which ancient empire?
A) Greek Empire
B) Roman Empire
C) Persian Empire
D) Egyptian Empire

970. Sumer was an ancient civilization located in the southern part of which region?
A) The Indus Valley
B) The Ganges Valley
C) The Nile Valley
D) Mesopotamia

971. The Austro-Hungarian Empire dissolved in which year?
A) 1914
B) 1918
C) 1920
D) 1939

972. The city of Angkor, known for its temples, was the capital of which empire?
A) Khmer Empire
B) Mongol Empire
C) Siamese Kingdom
D) Majapahit Empire

973. The ancient city of Mohenjo-daro was part of which civilization?
A) Mesopotamian Civilization
B) Egyptian Civilization
C) Indus Valley Civilization
D) Chinese Civilization

974. Which empire was centered in the city of Cuzco before the Spanish conquest?
A) Aztec Empire
B) Maya Civilization
C) Inca Empire
D) Olmec Civilization

975. The ancient city of Teotihuacan, known for its pyramids, was located in which modern-day country?
A) Mexico
B) Guatemala
C) Peru
D) Egypt

976. The Kingdom of Kush was an ancient civilization located along which river?
A) The Nile River
B) The Tigris River
C) The Euphrates River
D) The Indus River

977. The city of Aksum, an important trading center, was located in which modern-day country?
A) Egypt
B) Ethiopia
C) Sudan
D) Kenya

978. Which empire was centered around the city of Constantinople after the fall of the Western Roman Empire?
A) Byzantine Empire
B) Ottoman Empire
C) Persian Empire
D) Holy Roman Empire

979. The Kingdom of Sardinia played a significant role in the unification of which country?
A) Germany
B) France
C) Greece
D) Italy

980. Which ancient city was famously known as the "City of a Thousand Pillars" and is located in modern-day Syria?
A) Damascus
B) Aleppo
C) Palmyra
D) Homs

981. The Hanseatic League, a medieval commercial and defensive confederation, was based in which part of Europe?
A) Southern Europe
B) Eastern Europe
C) Western Europe
D) Northern Europe

982. Which modern city was previously named Lutetia by the Romans?
A) Barcelona
B) London
C) Paris
D) Bordeaux

983. The Minoan Civilization was centered on which Greek island?
A) Crete
B) Rhodes
C) Mykonos
D) Santorini

Section 17: Economies Of The World

984. What was the GDP of the United States in 2022?
A) $25 trillion
B) $20 trillion
C) $15 trillion
D) $10 trillion

985. What is the largest industry in China?
A) Agriculture
B) Manufacturing
C) Technology
D) Services

986. Which country had the highest inflation rate in 2022?
A) Venezuela
B) Zimbabwe
C) Argentina
D) Turkey

987. What is Japan's major export product?
A) Electronics
B) Automobiles
C) Textiles
D) Seafood

988. Which country has the largest oil reserves?
A) Saudi Arabia
B) Russia
C) Canada
D) Venezuela

989. What was India's GDP growth rate?
A) 7%
B) 5%
C) 9%
D) 3%

990. Which country had the lowest unemployment rate in 2022?
A) Japan
B) Germany
C) Qatar
D) Switzerland

991. Which country is known for being the largest exporter of coffee?
A) Colombia
B) Brazil
C) Vietnam
D) Ethiopia

992. What is South Korea's largest export commodity?
A) Steel
B) Automobiles
C) Semiconductors
D) Smartphones

993. What is the major industry in Australia?
A) Mining
B) Agriculture
C) Technology
D) Tourism

994. Who is France's biggest export partner?
A) United States
B) United Kingdom
C) Germany
D) China

995. Which country has the largest natural gas reserves?
A) Russia
B) Iran
C) Qatar
D) United States

996. What is Nigeria's main export?
A) Cocoa
B) Oil
C) Rubber
D) Gold

997. What is the major sector in the Canadian economy?
A) Energy
B) Agriculture
C) Manufacturing
D) Services

998. Which country has the highest per capita income?
A) United States
B) Switzerland
C) Norway
D) Luxembourg

999. Which is the largest economy in Africa by GDP?
A) Nigeria
B) South Africa
C) Egypt
D) Algeria

1000. What is the main industry in Italy?
A) Fashion
B) Automobiles
C) Wine production
D) Machinery

1001. Which country has the largest gold reserves?
A) United States
B) Germany
C) Italy
D) France

1002. What is Turkey's main export commodity?
  A) Textiles
  B) Automobiles
  C) Electronics
  D) Agriculture products

1003. What is Egypt's main source of foreign income?
  A) Tourism
  B) Oil exports
  C) Suez Canal fees
  D) Agriculture

1004. What is the largest sector in the UK economy?
  A) Manufacturing
  B) Services
  C) Agriculture
  D) Technology

1005. Which country has the highest trade surplus?
  A) China
  B) Germany
  C) Japan
  D) Russia

1006. What is Spain's largest industry?
  A) Tourism
  B) Agriculture
  C) Automobiles
  D) Textiles

1007. What is the major export of Indonesia?
  A) Textiles
  B) Rubber
  C) Palm oil
  D) Coffee

1008.What was Germany's largest export in 2022?
   A) Machinery
   B) Vehicles
   C) Pharmaceuticals
   D) Electrical equipment

1009.Which country had the highest number of billionaires in 2022?
   A) United States
   B) China
   C) India
   D) Russia

1010.What is Argentina's main agricultural export?
   A) Corn
   B) Wheat
   C) Beef
   D) Soybeans

1011.What was the United Kingdom's GDP as a percentage of the EU's total GDP (pre-Brexit)?
   A) 5%
   B) 10%
   C) 15%
   D) 20%

1012.Which sector is leading in Israel's economy?
   A) Agriculture
   B) Technology
   C) Tourism
   D) Manufacturing

1013.Which country has the largest diamond reserves?
   A) Russia
   B) Botswana
   C) Canada
   D) Australia

1014. What is New Zealand's top export commodity?
  A) Dairy products
  B) Meat
  C) Wool
  D) Wine

1015. What is the major source of revenue for the UAE?
  A) Tourism
  B) Oil exports
  C) Real estate
  D) Financial services

1016. Which country has the highest proportion of renewable energy in its total energy mix?
  A) Denmark
  B) Norway
  C) Sweden
  D) Iceland

1017. Among the following, which African country had the highest GDP in 2022?
  A) Egypt
  B) South Africa
  C) Nigeria
  D) Morocco

1018. Which of the following countries in the Americas had the highest GDP in 2022?
  A) Mexico
  B) Canada
  C) Brazil
  D) Argentina

1019. Which Middle Eastern country had the highest GDP?
- A) Saudi Arabia
- B) United Arab Emirates
- C) Israel
- D) Turkey

1020. Which Southeast Asian country has the highest GDP?
- A) Singapore
- B) Thailand
- C) Malaysia
- D) Indonesia

Section 18: National Parks

1021. Which national park is known for its geothermal features like Old Faithful?
A) Yosemite National Park
B) Yellowstone National Park
C) Zion National Park
D) Grand Canyon National Park

1022. In which country is Banff National Park located?
A) United States
B) Canada
C) Norway
D) New Zealand

1023. What is the main attraction of Serengeti National Park?
A) Glaciers
B) Coral Reefs
C) Annual Migration of Wildebeest
D) Mountain Ranges

1024. Which of these national parks is known for its fjords?
A) Kruger National Park
B) Fiordland National Park
C) Everglades National Park
D) Galápagos National Park

1025. Which national park in Africa is renowned for the Victoria Falls?
A) Kruger National Park
B) Serengeti National Park
C) Mosi-oa-Tunya National Park
D) Kilimanjaro National Park

1026. The Grand Canyon National Park is primarily located in which U.S. state?
A) Utah
B) Arizona
C) Colorado
D) Nevada

1027. Keoladeo National Park, famous for its bird sanctuary, is located in which country?
A) India
B) Brazil
C) South Africa
D) Canada

1028. Which national park in the United States is known for its volcanic landscapes and the deepest lake in the country, Crater Lake?
A) Yellowstone National Park
B) Mount Rainier National Park
C) Yosemite National Park
D) Crater Lake National Park

1029. Tanzania's Kilimanjaro National Park is famous for what natural feature?
A) The world's largest desert
B) Unique coral reefs
C) A vast savannah ecosystem
D) The highest free-standing mountain

1030. Which national park in the United States is known for its diverse wildlife and the Teton mountain range?
A) Yellowstone National Park
B) Grand Teton National Park
C) Yosemite National Park
D) Glacier National Park

1031. What is the main attraction of Kakadu National Park in Australia?
A) Snow-capped mountains
B) Rainforests and Aboriginal rock art
C) Hot springs
D) Large canyons

1032. Galápagos National Park, known for its unique wildlife, is part of which country?
A) Ecuador
B) Peru
C) Chile
D) Brazil

1033. Which national park in India is famous for its Bengal tiger population?
A) Keoladeo National Park
B) Ranthambore National Park
C) Jim Corbett National Park
D) Kaziranga National Park

1034. What unique feature is Skaftafell in Vatnajökull National Park in Iceland known for?
A) Geysers
B) Hot springs
C) Volcanic landscapes
D) Ice caves and glaciers

1035. Torres del Paine National Park, famous for its granite towers, is located in which country?
A) Argentina
B) Bolivia
C) Chile
D) Peru

1036. Which U.S. national park is known for its below-ground cave system with more than 400 miles explored?
A) Carlsbad Caverns National Park
B) Great Basin National Park
C) Mammoth Cave National Park
D) Wind Cave National Park

1037. Kruger National Park, a significant wildlife reserve, is in which country?
A) Kenya
B) South Africa
C) Botswana
D) Tanzania

1038. In which national park would you find the Half Dome and El Capitan granite formations?
A) Zion National Park
B) Yosemite National Park
C) Sequoia National Park
D) Rocky Mountain National Park

1039. Which national park in the United States is famous for its unique arch formations?
A) Arches National Park
B) Canyonlands National Park
C) Redwood National Park
D) Joshua Tree National Park

1040. Where is Plitvice Lakes National Park, known for its terraced lakes and waterfalls, located?
A) Croatia
B) Slovenia
C) Austria
D) Switzerland

1041. Mount Rainier National Park, famous for its active volcano, is in which U.S. state?
A) Washington
B) Oregon
C) California
D) Alaska

1042. What is the main feature of Bialowieza Forest, a national park straddling Poland and Belarus?
A) The largest mountain range in Europe
B) The oldest and largest primeval forest
C) Extensive cave systems
D) Geothermal hot springs

1043. Which national park in Costa Rica is known for its biodiversity and primary rainforest?
A) Manuel Antonio National Park
B) Corcovado National Park
C) Monteverde Cloud Forest Reserve
D) Arenal Volcano National Park

1044. The famous Christ the Redeemer statue overlooks which national park in Brazil?
A) Amazon National Park
B) Chapada Diamantina National Park
C) Tijuca National Park
D) Iguaçu National Park

1045. Which national park in South Africa is famous for its dramatic coastal cliffs and is the southernmost point of the African continent?
A) Kruger National Park
B) Addo Elephant National Park
C) Table Mountain National Park
D) Agulhas National Park

1046. In which country is Jasper National Park, known for its glaciers, lakes, and mountains, located?
A) Canada
B) United States
C) Norway
D) Switzerland

1047. Which national park is known as the first national park in the world, designated in 1872?
A) Yosemite National Park
B) Yellowstone National Park
C) Banff National Park
D) Kruger National Park

1048. Which national park in Australia is famous for the Uluru/Ayers Rock monolith?
A) Kakadu National Park
B) Great Barrier Reef Marine Park
C) Uluru-Kata Tjuta National Park
D) Royal National Park

1049. The Sundarbans National Park, known for its mangrove forests and Bengal tigers, is located in which two countries?
A) India and Nepal
B) Nepal and Bangladesh
C) India and Bhutan
D) Bangladesh and India

1050. Which national park in the United States is renowned for its underground labyrinth of caves?
A) Mammoth Cave National Park
B) Lassen Volcanic National Park
C) Wind Cave National Park
D) Carlsbad Caverns National Park

1051.In which country is the Doñana National Park, a wetland
famous for its birdlife, located?
A) Portugal
B) Cuba
C) Mexico
D) Spain

1052.Which national park in Canada is known for its rugged
coastline and marine wildlife?
A) Jasper National Park
B) Banff National Park
C) Pacific Rim National Park Reserve
D) Gros Morne National Park

1053.Gunung Leuser National Park, known for its orangutan
conservation, is in which Asian country?
A) Malaysia
B) Indonesia
C) Thailand
D) Vietnam

1054.Which national park in the United States is known for its giant
ancient trees, including the General Sherman tree?
A) Yosemite National Park
B) Sequoia National Park
C) Redwood National and State Parks
D) Kings Canyon National Park

1055.The Virunga National Park, known for its mountain gorillas, is
located in which African country?
A) Rwanda
B) Uganda
C) Democratic Republic of the Congo
D) Tanzania

1056. Where is the Wadden Sea National Park, known for its tidal flats and wetlands, not located?
A) Denmark
B) The Netherlands
C) Germany
D) Sweden

1057. Pantanal Conservation Area, one of the world's largest tropical wetland areas, is primarily located in which country?
A) Brazil
B) Bolivia
C) Paraguay
D) Argentina

Answers

Capital Cities

1. B) Paris
2. C) Tokyo
3. A) Ottawa
4. C) Canberra
5. D) Johannesburg
6. B) Washington D.C.
7. D) London
8. A) Brasília
9. C) Rome
10. C) New Delhi
11. D) Berlin
12. D) Cairo
13. D) Madrid
14. B) Moscow
15. C) Beijing
16. A) Buenos Aires
17. D) Bangkok
18. D) Seoul
19. C) Mexico City
20. B) Stockholm
21. B) Ankara
22. D) Abuja
23. C) Oslo
24. D) Tehran
25. C) Jakarta
26. C) Nairobi
27. A) Amsterdam
28. A) Kuala Lumpur
29. C) Wellington
30. C) Hanoi
31. D) Athens
32. D) Bern
33. B) Lisbon
34. D) Riyadh
35. C) Brussels
36. D) Bogotá

37. D) Lima
38. B) Warsaw
39. C) Helsinki
40. A) Copenhagen
41. D) Manila
42. C) Dublin
43. D) Dhaka
44. C) Santiago
45. D) Vienna
46. C) Juba
47. D) Kyiv
48. A) Ulaanbaatar
49. C) Havana
50. B) Islamabad
51. D) Bucharest
52. D) Kathmandu
53. A) Budapest
54. C) Bratislava
55. B) Zagreb
56. D) Minsk
57. C) Colombo
58. D) Prague
59. C) Rabat
60. C) Suva
61. D) Sofia
62. D) Beirut
63. B) Amman
64. A) Belgrade
65. A) Tallinn
66. D) Vilnius
67. D) Sarajevo
68. A) Montevideo
69. C) Nur-Sultan
70. D) Damascus
71. D) Tashkent
72. C) Reykjavík
73. C) Yerevan
74. D) Tbilisi
75. B) Doha
76. D) Vientiane
77. C) Manama

78. D) Tirana
79. C) Ljubljana
80. D) Nicosia
81. B) Valletta
82. C) Luxembourg City
83. D) Muscat
84. C) Baku
85. D) Asunción
86. C) Lusaka
87. A) Accra
88. D) Sucre
89. D) Santo Domingo
90. C) Tripoli
91. D) Quito
92. B) Lisbon
93. A) Dodoma
94. D) Riga
95. D) San José
96. C) San Salvador
97. D) Tegucigalpa
98. C) Ouagadougou
99. B) Yaoundé
100. C) Sacramento
101. B) Austin
102. C) Tallahassee
103. C) Albany
104. B) Springfield
105. A) Denver
106. C) Olympia
107. A) Boston
108. B) Phoenix
109. A) Atlanta
110. C) Harrisburg
111. D) Columbus
112. C) Lansing
113. C) Salem
114. B) Baton Rouge

Rivers & Lakes

115. B) India
116. A) Seine
117. B) Ethiopia
118. D) Rio Grande
119. D) Black Sea
120. A) Orinoco
121. B) California and Nevada
122. B) China
123. C) Niger River
124. A) Illinois
125. C) Caspian Sea
126. D) Mekong River
127. B) Russia
128. B) Tigris
129. C) Northwest Territories
130. D) Spain
131. B) Lake Nicaragua
132. A) Atlantic Ocean
133. B) Colorado River
134. D) Lake Superior
135. D) Chicago River
136. B) Zambezi River
137. A) Israel
138. C) Ethiopia
139. B) Bolivia and Peru
140. B) Nile River
141. C) Yellow River (Huang He)
142. D) Cambodia
143. B) Russia
144. A) Colorado River
145. B) Australia
146. A) Danube
147. D) 20%
148. B) Pakistan
149. C) Great Salt Lake
150. C) Vietnam
151. B) Rhône River
152. A) Iraq
153. D) Lake Victoria

154. A) Caspian Sea
155. B) Scotland
156. B) Ubangi River
157. D) Ethiopia
158. C) Hinduism
159. D) Manitoba
160. C) Washington, D.C.

Mountains & Mountain Ranges

161. B) South America
162. A) Canada and the United States
163. C) Movement of tectonic plates
164. B) The Himalayas
165. B) Japan
166. D) United States
167. A) K2
168. A) The Ural Mountains
169. B) The Caucasus Mountains
170. D) South Africa
171. A) The Andes
172. C) Volcanic Mountains
173. B) Italy
174. C) Northern Africa
175. B) The Andes
176. A) Mount McKinley (Denali)
177. D) The Karakoram
178. B) United States
179. B) Vinson Massif
180. A) France and Spain
181. C) Glaciers
182. A) Poland and Slovakia
183. B) The Apennines
184. C) The Black Hills
185. D) Ama Dablam
186. B) Australia
187. B) Greece
188. D) Bulgaria
189. B) Ben Nevis
190. A) Mount Elbrus

191. B) Turkey
192. B) The Rocky Mountains
193. A) The Andes
194. A) Yukon
195. B) Australia
196. D) Belgium
197. A) Mount Aconcagua
198. C) The Snowy Mountains
199. D) Russia
200. C) Big Island of Hawaii
201. C) The Ruwenzori Range
202. A) Alaska
203. B) Pakistan and Afghanistan
204. B) Cape Town
205. C) France and Italy
206. D) Mexico
207. D) Stratovolcano
208. B) Mount Mitchell
209. A) Savage Mountain
210. A) Mount Aconcagua
211. D) The Caucasus
212. A) Mount Cook (Aoraki)
213. A) Mount Vinson
214. B) Alaska
215. B) Toubkal
216. D) Mount Elbert
217. C) The Himalayas
218. A) Mount Kilimanjaro
219. A) Mont Blanc
220. D) Oceania
221. B) Honshu
222. C) Aconcagua
223. A) Mount Whitney
224. D) Meru
225. A) Mount Whitney

Climate Zones

226. C) Tropical Rainforest
227. B) Temperate

228. A) Subtropical
229. D) Low temperatures and sparse vegetation
230. D) Hot, dry summers and mild, wet winters
231. B) Desert
232. C) Near the Arctic and Antarctic Circles
233. C) Severe winters and warm summers
234. B) Tundra
235. B) Heavy rain in the summer and dry weather in the winter
236. B) Hot, dry summers and cold winters
237. C) Polar
238. C) Shrubs and woodlands
239. B) Prolonged dry seasons and short wet seasons
240. C) Tropical Rainforest
241. B) Warm to hot summers and cool to mild winters
242. D) Polar
243. D) Subarctic
244. B) Mediterranean
245. A) Polar
246. D) Desert
247. C) Highland
248. C) Oceanic
249. A) Humid Subtropical
250. B) Humid Subtropical
251. A) Highland
252. C) Subarctic
253. A) Desert
254. A) Highland
255. C) Monsoon
256. C) Desert
257. D) Oceanic
258. C) Tropical Rainforest
259. B) Subarctic
260. B) Desert

Cultural Geography

261. B) Spain
262. B) Japan
263. B) Germany
264. C) India

265. C) Danish
266. B) Rio de Janeiro
267. A) Maori
268. D) Japan
269. B) France
270. C) Portuguese
271. C) The South
272. B) Kenya and Tanzania
273. C) Indonesia
274. B) Portugal
275. C) The Arctic
276. D) Japan
277. D) Antwerp
278. D) India
279. B) Paris
280. B) Peru
281. A) Jamaica
282. C) Russian
283. B) Venice
284. C) South Korea
285. B) Paris
286. B) Germany
287. D) Egypt
288. A) Japan
289. C) Paris
290. C) England
291. B) Spain
292. C) Canada
293. C) Australia
294. A) Scotland
295. D) Italy
296. B) Athens
297. C) South Korea
298. C) Cuban
299. D) Germany
300. B) Brazil
301. C) Japan
302. B) Guangdong (Canton)
303. C) Norway
304. B) Peru
305. C) Argentina and Uruguay

Population & Demographics

306. A) Urbanization
307. A) Asia
308. B) Age and sex distribution of a population
309. D) Fertility rate
310. A) Population density
311. B) China
312. A) Decrease in skilled labor due to migration
313. B) 1.4 billion
314. B) United States
315. B) Germany
316. C) Nigeria
317. B) 37 million
318. D) Finland
319. A) South Korea
320. C) Brazil
321. A) Delhi
322. C) 8-10 million
323. B) South Asia
324. D) 1.4 billion
325. A) Sydney
326. C) São Paulo, Brazil
327. A) New York City
328. B) 450 million
329. A) Lagos, Nigeria
330. D) 350 million
331. B) India
332. D) Nigeria
333. B) 650 million
334. D) Suriname
335. C) 40 million
336. B) Nigeria
337. B) Africa
338. B) India
339. A) South Korea
340. A) North America
341. C) 8 billion
342. D) Monaco
343. C) Bulgaria
344. B) 55%

345. C) United Arab Emirates
346. D) Uruguay
347. D) About 60%
348. B) Ethiopia
349. D) Sweden
350. B) 1-2 million
351. A) Dubai

Languages & Religions Of The World

352. D) Portuguese
353. B) Hebrew
354. C) Mandarin Chinese
355. B) Kenya
356. C) Germanic
357. A) Russian
358. A) German
359. C) Mandarin Chinese
360. B) Finnish
361. A) India
362. B) Farsi (Persian)
363. D) Spanish
364. B) South Africa
365. A) Arabic
366. C) Tagalog
367. B) Spanish
368. B) Tanzania
369. C) Japanese
370. C) German
371. A) Saudi Arabia
372. C) Quechua
373. D) English
374. A) Cree
375. A) India
376. C) Persian (Dari)
377. C) Korean
378. A) Amharic
379. D) Urdu
380. D) Romansh

381. C) Mexico
382. B) France and Spain
383. C) Spain
384. A) Hindi
385. B) French
386. A) Nahuatl
387. C) Philippines
388. B) Egypt
389. D) Dutch
390. C) Hinduism
391. C) India
392. B) Vatican City
393. C) Japan
394. C) Indonesia
395. A) India
396. B) China
397. B) Germany
398. A) United States
399. B) Greece
400. D) Persian Empire
401. D) Ethiopia
402. B) United Kingdom
403. C) Tibet
404. B) Jamaica
405. A) Iran
406. C) Sweden
407. C) China
408. D) Buddhism

Geology & Landforms

409. D) Basalt
410. B) Asia
411. B) Mountain
412. C) Lake
413. C) Moon's gravitational pull
414. B) Active Volcanoes
415. B) Plate Tectonics
416. C) Movement of tectonic plates
417. C) Carbon Dioxide

418. A) Crust
419. C) Moon
420. A) Epicenter
421. C) Mouth of a river
422. D) Rainforest
423. B) Frozen water
424. C) Escarpment
425. B) Nitrogen
426. C) Earth's tilt on its axis
427. A) El Niño
428. C) Lithosphere
429. C) Temperature differences
430. A) Deep, narrow sea inlet bordered by steep cliffs
431. C) Erosion
432. A) A large naturally occurring community of flora and fauna
433. A) Wind patterns
434. A) Watershed
435. C) A large, flat-topped hill or mountain
436. A) Aurora Borealis and Aurora Australis
437. B) Butte
438. D) Prairie
439. C) River erosion
440. C) Isthmus
441. A) Ring-shaped coral reefs, islands, or series of islets
442. B) A deep, bowl-shaped landform
443. B) Plateau
444. C) River
445. B) Deep inlet of the sea almost surrounded by land, with a narrow mouth
446. B) A ridge of jagged rock, coral, or sand just above or below the surface of the sea
447. A) Continent
448. B) A deep gorge, typically one with a river flowing through it
449. C) A group or chain of islands clustered together in a sea or ocean
450. B) Fjord
451. A) Narrow body of water that connects two larger bodies of water
452. A) A narrow strip of land with sea on either side, forming a link between two larger areas of land
453. A) A shallow body of water separated from a larger body of water by barrier islands or reefs
454. D) A piece of land that juts out into the sea; a headland

455. A) Cliff
456. A) A fertile spot in a desert where water is found
457. A) Delta
458. B) A mass of rocks and sediment carried down and deposited by a glacier
459. A) Strait
460. C) Igneous
461. B) Oxygen
462. C) Sedimentary
463. A) Igneous
464. C) Metamorphic
465. C) Compaction and cementation
466. C) Granite
467. B) Limestone
468. C) Limestone
469. B) Banding or stripes
470. A) Quartz
471. C) Sedimentary
472. B) Extrusive
473. D) Its layering
474. A) Tuff
475. C) Limestone

Seas & Oceans

476. C) 71%
477. C) Gravitational pull of the Moon and Sun
478. B) Shallow, tropical waters
479. D) Absorption of CO_2 from the atmosphere
480. B) Nitrogen
481. C) Plankton
482. D) Thermohaline Circulation
483. A) El Niño
484. D) Stratospheric
485. C) Philippine Sea
486. D) Dead Sea
487. A) It has no coastline
488. B) Upwelling
489. A) Adriatic Sea

490. A) Coral Sea
491. A) Arabian Sea
492. A) Calypso Deep
493. B) Israel
494. B) Barents Sea
495. D) It's the world's largest lake
496. D) Caribbean Sea
497. A) China
498. B) Caspian Sea
499. C) Mediterranean Sea and Black Sea
500. A) Mediterranean Sea
501. B) Canada
502. B) Sea of Azov
503. C) United States and Russia
504. D) Sargasso Sea
505. B) Mediterranean Sea
506. A) Black Sea
507. B) China and South Korea
508. C) Arabian Sea
509. A) Indian Ocean
510. B) The Moon
511. B) Baltic Sea
512. A) Arabian Sea
513. A) Aegean Sea
514. C) Antarctica
515. D) Ionian Sea
516. A) Atlantic Ocean
517. B) Aegean Sea
518. C) Italy
519. A) Kattegat
520. D) Indian Ocean
521. A) Southern Ocean
522. D) Atlantic Ocean
523. B) Pacific Ocean
524. A) Arctic Ocean
525. C) Atlantic Ocean
526. C) Pacific Ocean
527. D) Indian Ocean
528. A) Atlantic Ocean
529. C) Indian Ocean
530. B) Pacific Ocean

531. D) Southern Ocean
532. B) Atlantic Ocean
533. A) Indian Ocean
534. C) Pacific Ocean
535. B) Java Sea
536. A) Arctic Ocean
537. D) Black Sea
538. B) New Zealand
539. A) Red Sea
540. A) Indian Ocean
541. B) Black Sea
542. D) Atlantic Ocean
543. C) South China Sea
544. A) Mediterranean Sea
545. D) North Atlantic Ocean
546. B) New Zealand
547. C) Pacific Ocean
548. A) Arabian Sea and Red Sea
549. A) Pacific Ocean
550. A) Adriatic Sea
551. B) South China Sea

Countries, Borders & Regions

552. B) Ethiopia
553. A) Africa
554. C) Turkey (Istanbul)
555. B) China
556. D) Lesotho
557. B) Norway
558. C) Nigeria
559. C) Germany
560. B) Norway
561. C) Ireland
562. A) Monaco
563. A) Japan
564. D) Denmark
565. D) China
566. C) Switzerland
567. B) Italy

568. A) Uruguay
569. C) United States
570. D) Romania
571. B) Italy
572. C) Australia
573. C) Canada and United States
574. B) South Africa
575. D) Ireland
576. A) China and Russia
577. B) Great Lakes
578. A) France and Spain
579. B) China
580. A) Zambia and Zimbabwe
581. A) North Korea and South Korea
582. C) France
583. A) Brazil and Argentina
584. A) Germany
585. B) Red Sea
586. D) Spain and Morocco
587. B) Nepal and China
588. C) Panama
589. C) Laos
590. B) Bass Strait
591. A) United States and Russia
592. B) Brahmaputra
593. C) Sudan and South Sudan
594. C) France and United Kingdom
595. C) China
596. B) States
597. C) India and China
598. D) Fences and fortifications
599. C) Andes Mountains
600. B) Switzerland
601. B) Provinces and Territories
602. A) States and Union Territories
603. B) Japan
604. A) Oblasts
605. A) States and Territories
606. D) States
607. B) France
608. B) Barcelona

609. A) Tuscany (Pisa)
610. B) Baden-Württemberg
611. D) Bordeaux
612. A) California
613. B) Queensland
614. B) Yorkshire
615. B) Pakistan
616. C) North Africa
617. B) Edmonton
618. A) Siberia
619. D) North
620. B) Shaanxi
621. B) Chubu
622. A) Rift Valley
623. A) Campania
624. B) Spain
625. A) Chile and Argentina
626. C) Centre-Val de Loire
627. D) Pennsylvania Dutch Country
628. A) Spain
629. B) Germany
630. A) Scotland
631. D) California
632. D) Western Australia
633. B) Limpopo
634. B) Portugal
635. C) Italy
636. D) The West Coast
637. A) Italy
638. D) Assam
639. B) Ecuador
640. B) France
641. A) Romania
642. C) North-West District
643. B) Turkey
644. B) England
645. D) Quintana Roo
646. D) Quebec
647. A) Arizona
648. C) New Brunswick
649. B) Yucatán

650. B) Florida
651. A) Prince Edward Island
652. A) Minnesota
653. A) British Columbia
654. A) Quebec
655. A) Nevada
656. B) Netherlands
657. C) United States and Russia
658. B) Libya and Chad
659. A) Botswana, Zambia, Zimbabwe, and Namibia
660. C) Spain
661. C) In the Pyrenees
662. A) Morocco
663. D) Switzerland
664. B) India and Pakistan
665. A) Canada
666. B) Canada and Denmark

Islands

667. A) Bali
668. A) Greenland
669. B) Easter Island
670. A) Corsica
671. C) Sicily
672. D) Komodo Island
673. C) Big Island (Hawaii)
674. B) Santorini
675. B) Hispaniola
676. C) Galapagos Islands
677. B) Australia
678. A) Iceland
679. C) Tenerife
680. A) Grenada
681. B) Cayman Islands
682. B) Borneo
683. C) Grande Terre
684. D) Bohol
685. B) Denpasar
686. B) Tanzania

687. D) Hawaii
688. B) Ireland
689. C) None, Troy is on the mainland
690. A) Oahu, Hawaii
691. B) South Korea
692. A) Indian Ocean
693. A) Great Britain
694. A) Ecuador
695. C) The Solomon Islands
696. A) Indian Ocean
697. A) Norway
698. B) Spain
699. C) Bermuda
700. C) Borneo
701. B) Greece
702. A) The Azores
703. D) 7,600
704. A) Chile
705. A) Indian Ocean
706. C) The Venetian Lagoon
707. B) Scotland
708. C) Denmark
709. D) Puerto Rico
710. A) Argentina and Chile
711. B) Africa
712. D) New Zealand
713. B) Tanzania
714. A) Canada
715. D) Japan
716. B) India
717. C) Tierra del Fuego
718. C) Scotland
719. B) Japan
720. C) France
721. B) Norway
722. B) Pacific Ocean
723. A) South China Sea

Cities, Buildings & Landmarks

724. B) Saint Basil's Cathedral
725. B) Athens
726. C) New York City
727. C) Agra
728. C) Rome
729. A) Dubai
730. B) San Francisco
731. C) Jordan
732. A) London
733. B) South Dakota
734. B) Chicago
735. C) England
736. D) Bangkok
737. D) Paris
738. C) Egypt
739. D) Moscow
740. B) San Francisco
741. D) Pisa
742. B) Cambodia
743. B) New York City
744. B) Venice
745. C) New York City
746. C) St. Petersburg
747. A) London
748. A) Amsterdam
749. B) Rio de Janeiro
750. C) St. Louis
751. C) New York City
752. C) Granada
753. D) Paris
754. D) Athens
755. D) Sydney
756. B) Istanbul
757. B) Madrid
758. A) Beijing
759. A) Paris
760. D) Zambia and Zimbabwe
761. B) Miami

762. D) Amsterdam
763. A) Beijing
764. C) Jerusalem
765. B) Seattle
766. C) France
767. B) London
768. C) Florence
769. A) Istanbul
770. C) Philadelphia
771. B) Ireland
772. B) Rome
773. C) Tokyo
774. B) Germany
775. C) Rio de Janeiro
776. B) Copenhagen
777. C) China
778. C) Bilbao
779. A) The Elizabeth Tower
780. D) Kuala Lumpur
781. B) White House
782. D) Delhi
783. C) London
784. D) Taipei
785. B) Chicago
786. C) New York City
787. D) Barcelona
788. C) Beijing
789. C) New York City
790. A) Toronto
791. D) Bastille
792. A) New York City
793. D) Mill Run, Pennsylvania
794. B) Brussels
795. A) Singapore
796. D) Washington D.C.
797. B) London
798. A) Lisbon
799. B) Bucharest
800. B) Riyadh
801. C) Hong Kong
802. A) London

803. C) Malmö
804. D) Mumbai
805. A) Berlin
806. B) Shanghai

Extreme Weather & Natural Disasters

807. D) Oceanic temperature rise
808. B) Fujita Scale
809. A) Drought
810. A) Tsunamis
811. B) Name based on location
812. D) Underwater volcanic eruption or earthquake
813. B) A storm with freezing rain
814. A) Troposphere
815. B) Location of formation
816. C) Oceanic temperature variations
817. C) Heavy snowfall
818. D) Along tectonic plate boundaries
819. D) Earthquakes or heavy rain
820. C) Carbon dioxide
821. B) Wind speed
822. C) Volcanic eruption
823. B) Strong winds in arid or semi-arid regions
824. D) Change in water temperature
825. B) Rapid flow of mud due to water saturation
826. D) Warm, moist air rising and cooling
827. D) Front
828. C) Saffir-Simpson Hurricane Wind Scale
829. B) Earthquakes
830. C) Underwater earthquakes or volcanic eruptions
831. B) A volcanic mudflow
832. D) Cumulonimbus
833. A) Powder snow avalanche
834. C) Natural weathering of limestone
835. A) Hurricane Katrina
836. B) Haiti
837. B) Sumatra, Indonesia
838. C) France

839. A) Washington
840. D) Great Plains
841. A) 2012
842. A) Mississippi River
843. B) Japan
844. A) 2009
845. A) Philippines
846. A) 1900
847. D) United Kingdom
848. D) San Francisco
849. B) Barometric pressure
850. B) Philippines
851. C) Myanmar
852. B) Missouri, Illinois, and Indiana
853. A) 1755
854. C) Iran
855. C) Honduras
856. B) Yangtze River
857. B) Australia
858. D) India
859. A) 1995
860. B) Colombia
861. C) Ethiopia
862. D) Victoria and South Australia
863. A) Guatemala
864. A) 1976

Deserts

865. B) Namib Desert
866. C) Wind patterns and geographical location
867. D) Sonoran Desert
868. B) Africa
869. C) Water conservation
870. C) Shrubs and cacti
871. A) Atacama Desert
872. A) China and Mongolia
873. C) Scarcity of water
874. D) Mojave Desert

875. B) Asia
876. B) Refraction of light
877. D) Lut Desert
878. C) Thick, water-storing stems
879. B) Karakum Desert
880. A) Atacama Desert
881. C) 10 inches
882. A) Atacama Desert
883. C) Australia
884. C) Fog and dew
885. B) Reduce water loss
886. D) Arabian Desert
887. D) United States and Mexico
888. B) Underground water sources
889. C) Joshua Tree
890. A) Mojave Desert
891. A) Gobi Desert
892. C) Mountain Desert
893. C) Gibson Desert
894. B) Gobi Desert
895. B) Unusually shaped chalk rock formations
896. D) Gobi Desert
897. B) Mojave Desert
898. C) Latitude

Geography World Records

899. B) Russia
900. B) Canada
901. A) Mariana Trench
902. C) Vatican City
903. B) Nile
904. D) Antarctic Desert
905. D) Mount Everest
906. C) Pacific Ocean
907. A) Lake Baikal
908. A) Finland
909. A) Greenland
910. B) Indonesia

911. D) Yangtze River
912. C) China
913. D) Dead Sea
914. D) Atacama Desert
915. A) The Andes
916. C) Great Barrier Reef
917. A) Monaco
918. B) Canada
919. D) Ojos del Salado
920. A) Arctic Ocean
921. A) Gulf of Mexico
922. A) Italy
923. B) Japan
924. D) Antarctica
925. B) United States
926. B) La Paz, Bolivia
927. C) Lake Victoria
928. C) Mid-Atlantic Ridge
929. A) Ganges-Brahmaputra Delta
930. A) Tokyo, Japan
931. D) France (including overseas territories)
932. B) Mount Etna
933. B) Amazon Rainforest
934. A) Amazon River
935. C) Angel Falls
936. C) Indonesia
937. A) Africa
938. B) Volga
939. D) Sweden
940. A) Arabian Peninsula
941. C) Tibetan Plateau
942. A) Bay of Bengal
943. B) Canada
944. A) Canada
945. B) Salar de Uyuni, Bolivia

Historical Countries & Cities

946. C) Florence
947. B) The Mongols

948. C) Troy
949. B) Mexico City
950. D) Istanbul
951. B) London
952. A) Mali
953. D) Tenochtitlan
954. B) Jordan
955. C) Phoenicians
956. B) Philadelphia
957. D) 1868
958. A) New Amsterdam
959. A) Inca Empire
960. B) Iraq
961. C) Greece
962. C) Istanbul
963. B) Ayutthaya
964. D) St. Petersburg
965. B) Manchester
966. B) India
967. C) 1945
968. D) Persian Empire
969. B) Roman Empire
970. D) Mesopotamia
971. B) 1918
972. A) Khmer Empire
973. C) Indus Valley Civilization
974. C) Inca Empire
975. A) Mexico
976. A) The Nile River
977. B) Ethiopia
978. A) Byzantine Empire
979. D) Italy
980. C) Palmyra
981. D) Northern Europe
982. C) Paris
983. A) Crete

Economies Of The World

984. A) $25 trillion
985. B) Manufacturing
986. A) Venezuela
987. B) Automobiles
988. D) Venezuela
989. A) 7%
990. C) Qatar
991. B) Brazil
992. C) Semiconductors
993. A) Mining
994. C) Germany
995. A) Russia
996. B) Oil
997. D) Services
998. D) Luxembourg
999. A) Nigeria
1000. D) Machinery
1001. A) United States
1002. A) Textiles
1003. C) Suez Canal fees
1004. B) Services
1005. A) China
1006. A) Tourism
1007. C) Palm oil
1008. B) Vehicles
1009. A) United States
1010. D) Soybeans
1011. C) 15%
1012. B) Technology
1013. B) Botswana
1014. A) Dairy products
1015. B) Oil exports
1016. D) Iceland
1017. C) Nigeria
1018. C) Brazil
1019. A) Saudi Arabia
1020. D) Indonesia

National Parks

1021. B) Yellowstone National Park
1022. B) Canada
1023. C) Annual Migration of Wildebeest
1024. B) Fiordland National Park
1025. C) Mosi-oa-Tunya National Park
1026. B) Arizona
1027. A) India
1028. D) Crater Lake National Park
1029. D) The highest free-standing mountain
1030. B) Grand Teton National Park
1031. B) Rainforests and Aboriginal rock art
1032. A) Ecuador
1033. B) Ranthambore National Park
1034. D) Ice caves and glaciers
1035. C) Chile
1036. C) Mammoth Cave National Park
1037. B) South Africa
1038. B) Yosemite National Park
1039. A) Arches National Park
1040. A) Croatia
1041. A) Washington
1042. B) The oldest and largest primeval forest
1043. B) Corcovado National Park
1044. C) Tijuca National Park
1045. D) Agulhas National Park
1046. A) Canada
1047. B) Yellowstone National Park
1048. C) Uluru-Kata Tjuta National Park
1049. D) Bangladesh and India
1050. D) Carlsbad Caverns National Park
1051. D) Spain
1052. C) Pacific Rim National Park Reserve
1053. B) Indonesia
1054. B) Sequoia National Park
1055. C) Democratic Republic of the Congo
1056. D) Sweden
1057. A) Brazil

Made in United States
Troutdale, OR
01/04/2024

16660184R00137